MEMORIAL VIGNETTE

THE PRESBYTERIAN MEMORIAL OFFERING

1870-1871

Presbyterian church in the U. S. A. General assembly. Presbyterian memorial committee.

New York:

DeWitt C. Lent and Company.

Committee on the Memorial Fund.

WINTHROP S. GILMAN,
JOHN CROSBY BROWN,
JOHN E. PARSONS,
ALEXANDER WHILLDIN,
BENJAMIN F. BUTLER,
WILLIAM T. BOOTH,
ARCHIBALD McCLURE, Jr.,
ISAAC SCARRITT,
GEORGE JUNKIN.

Officers of the Committee.

WINTHROP S. GILMAN, *Chairman.*
Hon. WILLIAM E. DODGE, *Treasurer.*
Rev. FRANK F. ELLINWOOD, D.D., *Corresponding Sec'y.*

ERRATA.

Page 36, fourth line from the top, read: "D. R. Campbell; General Objects, $55,000.00; Total, $94,900.00."

The footings should read: "Home Objects, $141,910.50; General Objects, $64,932.10; Total, $206,842.60."

Page 40, sixth line from the bottom, read: "C. H. Perkins."

Page 41, seventh line from the bottom, read: "F. Brown."

Page 44, tenth line from the bottom, read: "D. X. Junkin, D.D."

PREFATORY NOTE.

IT cannot be expected that the statistics of the Memorial Report will be found to be entirely accurate. Had all returns from the churches been made in the forms which were furnished, entire accuracy would have been attainable; but with the imperfect reports which have been received—often omitting even to name the Presbytery from which they came, and giving partial amounts at different times—the Committee have by great labor endeavored to reach the nearest possible approximations.

In some instance where churches have been credited with amounts given by individuals to colleges or poor churches, and not reported by their own officers, the total will be found larger than the original reports. In other cases the original reports have been diminished on account of a reported failure to reach the amount at first subscribed.

The amount of additional reports rendered subsequent to the meeting of the Assembly is a little less than a quarter of a million of dollars, being made up mostly of small returns from the country churches.

The Committee, understanding that the extension of time by the Assembly till the 1st of August was intended only to admit reports which were designed to be given before the Assembly, have put forth no effort to swell the amount, but have merely entered what was reported up to the allotted time.

The total up to August 1st lacks a little of *Eight Millions of Dollars.*

As there is in the body of the report rendered to the Assembly some allusion to various sums raised in the churches which, to the amount of two millions at least, were excluded from the Memorial footings, it may be well to state more definitely on what grounds that estimate was based.

In the correspondence of the churches during the year amounts were often named as being expended in various ways, but which the donors did not choose to consider Memorial.

The Secretary of the Committee kept an account of these *outside expenditures*, reaching at least from two to three millions of dollars, which might properly have been included within the limits prescribed. It may be proper to state, as showing the real strength of the church, that of the immense expenditures upon the Presbyterian Hospital in New York, not over $50,000 was reported in the Memorial Fund. For the hospital in Philadelphia, also valued at a very large sum, not over $20,000 was counted Memorial. Of the noble gifts made to Princeton College only about $30,000 was included, and about $10,000 of the amount raised for the Theological Seminary. One hundred thousand dollars given by one individual to a local institution in Western Pennsylvania was not reported, and the same may be said of considerable sums given within the limits of the Synod of New York for different seminaries and colleges.

Extensive church building operations in various sections of the Church were excluded from the report; and while many cancelled debts and needed repairs were reported, many more were left out of the account.

Even where the Memorial work has not been approved, it has at the same time been *emulated*, so that the kingdom of Christ has been everywhere advanced.

There may have been disappointment among the friends of some of our institutions of learning at not having received larger endowments during this common effort.

It will be seen, however, from the above statements, that the aggregate raised by the Church for this class of institutions during the Memorial period is more than *Two Millions of Dollars.*

The tabular report herewith published is designed to show only the gifts of churches as such. It is found to be impossible to publish the gifts of individuals, which, therefore, are simply entered on the permanent books of the Committee.

In consequence a very large balance is herein presented under the general head of "Miscellaneous." Some of the very largest and noblest of all the Memorial offerings are embraced in it, but it is impossible to discriminate between donors.

The complete manuscript records of all the churches, with their gifts or failures, were presented for general inspection at the meeting of the Assembly; but in this final printed form only the contributing churches are recorded.

PREAMBLES AND RESOLUTIONS PRESENTED BY REV. SAMUEL W. FISHER, D.D., LL.D., AND ADOPTED IN JOINT CONVENTION BY THE MEMBERS OF THE TWO ASSEMBLIES, PITTSBURGH, NOVEMBER 12, 1869.

IN the Providence of God, the two Branches of the Presbyterian Church in the United States of America, after a separation of more than thirty years, are again united. This event, in its magnitude, is unparalleled in the ecclesiastical history of this country, and almost of the world. It evidences to all men the presence and unifying power of the Divine Spirit. A fact so remarkable and significant attracts interest and creates expectation among even worldly minds. It awakens the sympathies and the hopes of all who truly love Christ among other denominations. It awakens hope, since it illustrates the evident purpose of God to bring all his followers into closer union in spirit, combine them in action for the overthrow of error and the diffusion of his truth; it awakens expectation, since they justly anticipate on our part, from this union of resources, spirit, and action, a far more vigorous assault upon the forces of darkness, and more decided efforts to spread the Gospel among all classes in our own and other lands.

To us, as a Church, it is an era in our history most memorable and hopeful; memorable, as it signalizes the triumph of faith and love over the strifes and jealousies of more than a quarter of a century; hopeful, since it is not the result of decadence and torpor, but of progress and augmented strength. It buries the suspicions and the rivalries of the past, with the sad necessity of magnifying our differences in order to justify our separation. It banishes the spirit of division, the natural foe of true progress. In this union are seen the outflashing of a divine purpose to lead us on to greater self-sacrifice, and a more entire consecration to the evangelization of the world. God has elevated us to this commanding position, that we may see His glory, and in the strengthened faith it inspires devote our united resources more directly and efficiently to the salvation of men. New and grander responsibilities rest upon us. Jesus summons us to a holier faith and more perfect consecration. He summons this Church to answer his loving kindness by deeds commensurate with our renewed resources. The times are auspicious; everywhere peace reigns; the gates are open, and the millions of our own and other lands wait for the Gospel. Our position is commanding; our resources great;

our methods of action well settled, simple, and efficient. The Spirit of God that has united us will inspire, direct, and bless our efforts. While we maintain the faith which Paul so fully unfolded, and our Church, in the centuries past, has, through manifold persecution and martyrdom, so gloriously upheld, we are summoned, as by the will of God, to arise and build, to form new, broader, and bolder plans for the extension of Christ's kingdom, and to enter upon and execute them with apostolic enthusiasm.

Let us, then, the ministers, elders, and members of this Church here assembled, as in spirit standing in the presence of and representing the entire body of believers in our connection, and the beloved missionaries in foreign lands, who now await with tender and prayerful interest this consummation of our union—let us, in humble dependence upon our dear Redeemer, with deep humility, in view of our past inefficiency and present unworthiness, and as an expression of our devout gratitude to Him who has brought this once dissevered, now united, Church up to this *Mount of Transfiguration*, signalize this most blessed and joyous *union* with an offering in some good degree commensurate with the abundant pecuniary gifts that He has bestowed on us. And, to this end, be it

Resolved, That it is incumbent on the Presbyterian Church in the United States of America, one in organization, one in faith, and one in effort, to make a special offering to the treasury of the Lord of Five Millions of Dollars: and we pledge ourselves, first of all, to seek in our daily petitions the blessing of God to make this resolution effectual; and second, that we will, with untiring perseverance and personal effort, endeavor to animate the whole Church with the purpose to secure the accomplishment of this great work before the third Thursday of May, 1871.

Resolved, further, That the Stated Clerks of the Assemblies of 1869 be requested to publish this paper, with the names of the Moderators, Clerks, the Joint Committee on Reunion, and the Commissioners now in attendance, appended thereto.

This action was by common understanding rather than by formal vote referred to the Joint Committee on Finance, and they were expected to report to the United Assembly in May, 1870, at Philadelphia.

The Joint Committee consisted of the following persons:—

Rev. John Hall, D.D.
Rev. Chas. K. Imbrie, D.D.
Hon. Robert McKnight.
Hon. Hovey K. Clarke.
Mr. W. S. Gilman.
Hon. William E. Dodge.
Hon. William Strong.
Rev. Jonathan F. Stearns, D.D.
Rev. William H. Goodrich, D.D.
Rev. Charles Hawley, D.D.

It was also understood that Hon. William E. Dodge should be authorized, as Treasurer of the Fund, to open books immediately for the receipt and recording of offerings.

Report of the Joint Committee on Finance relating to the Memorial Fund, as Amended and Adopted by the General Assembly at Philadelphia, May, 1870.

The Joint Committee was called into existence by the following resolution of the Joint Committee on Reunion :—

"*Resolved*, That a Committee of five from each branch of the Church be appointed to take into consideration the subject of raising funds for the use of the United Church, and the best methods of doing the same, and the objects to which the same should be directed, and to report to the next General Assembly."

The Convention of the United Churches at Pittsburgh, Pa., further agreed, with enthusiasm, to the following resolution :—

"*Resolved*, That it is incumbent on the Presbyterian Church of the United States of America, one in organization, one in faith, and one in effort, to make a special offering to the treasury of the Lord, of Five Millions of Dollars: and we pledge ourselves, first of all, to seek in our daily petitions the blessing of God to make this resolution effectual; and second, that we will, with untiring perseverance and personal effort, endeavor to animate the whole Church with the purpose to secure the accomplishment of this great work before the third Thursday of May, 1871."

The action of the Committee upon these resolutions is herewith submitted.

On the subject of the Five Million Memorial Fund, the Joint-Committee (all the members being present but two, who were hindered by unavoidable engagements), after most careful and anxious deliberation, agreed unanimously upon the following resolutions :—

1. That, notwithstanding we find, on examination, that the terms of the resolution adopted on the subject by the General Assemblies recently met at Pittsburgh, Pa., do not distinctly enjoin the duty of raising the proposed "Memorial Fund" upon this Joint Committee; yet, being fully persuaded that the general voice and expectation of the Church have determined that this service fairly belongs to the Committee; and, further, inasmuch as funds for this object have already been tendered to us, we assume this to be a duty embraced within the intention of the Assemblies in our appointment; and therefore we conclude to initiate this work at once, and to conduct it until the meeting of the General Assembly.

2. That, in the judgment of this Joint Committee, it is not within the intention of the Church to include in this fund the ordinary contributions to the Church's stated work (which in our new position should be greatly advanced), but to create and strengthen permanent institutions at home and abroad, to meet such extraordinary claims as arise out of our new position, and to effect such objects as properly commemorate our union. By these we mean—

I. Theological seminaries, colleges, and seminaries for the education of our daughters, including buildings and endowments of the same; it being understood that such institutions shall be chartered, and shall be in connection with the Presbyterian Church.

II. Literary institutions for the raising of a native Gospel ministry in heathen lands.

III. Church buildings and manses originating subsequently to the Union, and otherwise entitled to public aid; hospitals and orphan asylums in connection with the Church.

IV. Institutions for the education and evangelization of Freedmen.

V. Special contributions for the establishment of a permanent Sustentation Fund, which shall include funds to be appropriated for the support of disabled ministers and their families.

At the same time the Committee announced that the Hon. William E. Dodge, as Treasurer, in accordance with the recommendation of the Convention, would receive donations for these objects, and donations to be applied hereafter, at the discretion of the General Assembly.

These resolutions were extensively published, and while much diversity of view appears to prevail regarding details, their leading principle appears to have secured general acceptance, and in various quarters efforts have been inaugurated in accordance with it.

The Committee having considered what practical measures should be suggested to the General Assembly, with a view to realizing the Five Million Memorial Fund before the third Thursday in May, 1871, according to a resolution of the Pittsburgh Convention,

It was unanimously agreed to recommend—

1st. The appointment of a Committee for the raising and disposition of this fund, subject to the principles now agreed upon.

2d. That this Committee shall examine the claims of particular institutions seeking to enjoy the benefit of the fund, either by direct appropriation or their own efforts, the results of which are reckoned as part of the fund.

3d. That, in addition to other efforts, a collection be made in all our congregations, as nearly simultaneously as practicable, during the month of January, 1871, when the ministers, having prepared the way by keeping the subject constantly before the people in the interval, shall more especially urge the contribution upon them.

4th. That the Committee, constituted by the first resolution, be instructed to prepare and forward to each congregation through the pastor, stated supply, or session, to be laid before each member of the congregation, a *clear*, *distinct*, and *minute* plan for *subscribing*, *reporting*, *collecting*, and *forwarding* the amounts contributed to this fund, and also to prepare and send suitable blanks for these purposes.

5th. That our Presbyteries and Synods be instructed, at their fall meetings, to make careful inquiry of each pastor and elder, and know if these subscriptions have been presented to the *individuals* of *all* our congregations; and in cases of failure to take such measures as may best secure this result.

The following Committee was appointed the Committee on the Memorial Fund:—

Messrs. Winthrop S. Gilman, J. Crosby Brown, John E. Parsons, Alexander Whilldin, Benjamin F. Butler, Isaac Scarritt, William T. Booth, Archibald McClure, Jr., and George Junkin.

Reception of the Memorial Report by the General Assembly at Chicago, May 23d, 1871.

At three o'clock on Tuesday afternoon, the order of the day receiving the report on the Memorial Fund was taken up. A considerable audience of ladies and gentlemen, besides that usually in attendence, had filled the house in all parts. Mr. Winthrop S. Gilman, of New York, the Chairman of the Committee, was introduced by the Moderator, amid applause, and said:—

I rise to make some explanation before the reading of the report. You gave us that privilege a day or two since, in the passage of the resolution to hear the report this afternoon. I want to say that in the progress of the work, we have, as a Committee, sometimes had our dark days, have met with much that is discouraging, and it seemed as though God, in His providence, was about to do with the Presbyterian Church, that which He often does in His wonder-working ways—disappoint the earnest expectation of His people, and cause them to feel humbled before Him by failure.

But as the work progressed, and when it came within five or

six weeks of completion, as we hoped, and we had less than a million of dollars upon our books, we at the same time lost all sense of apprehension. The view we had of the feeling throughout the union; the evidences of the influences of the Holy Spirit touching one heart and another, were so manifest that we lost all anxiety, and rested in the hands of God, perfectly willing. I speak on behalf of my brethren and myself when I say that we were perfectly willing that it should be but three or four millions of dollars, if God so pleased. If you could look into the correspondence that has come before the Committee, you would see in the incidents—the repeated incidents of the greatest interest, especially among the poor, the offerings of the poor, their prayers and their self-denial—you would see that which would lead you to say that the salt of a divine savor was bestowed upon it in answer to our prayers. And especially I would congratulate you, my brethren, that in the first act of the reunited body we agreed that it was incumbent upon the Presbyterian Church to make a special offering of Five Millions of Dollars to the treasury of the Lord, and the saving clause was put in: "And we pledge ourselves in our daily prayers to seek the blessing of God that this resolution may be effectual." It is the prayers—the widow's prayers, the orphan's prayers, the prayers of the poor—their self-denial, and the combined influence of the whole Church, that have brought this act to its consummation. And it teaches us a very great lesson in the spiritual profit to the Church. The whole interest concentrates, to my mind, in this fact—the spiritual benefit to the Church of God.

I will not go on with any incidents, though they are very moving, for I know you are impatient to hear the report. I will only mention the rigid course that this Committee has taken in counting the offerings of the Church. In many cases clergymen have sent us a report stating: "We have contributed so much for general purposes, so much for our home objects," and below the signature would be found written, "And we have also paid $7,000 on a church debt which you may count in if you see proper." No, no, my friends, it is the intent of the giver that bestows the Memorial quality, and we have acted upon the principle that if the Church felt any doubt whether they consecreated it to Christ we would mark it off, and we have laid aside many and many such subscriptions. Again, in the great variety of views entertained by individuals in making a free-will offering to God, of course there would be a vast number of offerings, just outside the line, which we could not count. I will instance one of them. A gentleman on the Hudson River wanted to make one of his princely donations in a Memorial gift of $30,000 to a theological seminary; but his interest concentrated chiefly in the theological seminary of Virginia, where our Southern brethren congregate. He gave it to that institution—claiming that it was a Memorial offering, acceptable, no doubt, to God, as anything in our treasury. But we could not count it. This was the Memorial offering of our own Church. (Applause.) I will not detain you longer (I know you must be impatient), only to introduce to you our Secretary, well known to all, the Rev. Dr. Ellinwood, who will now read the report; and you will be assured by it that the Church has fulfilled her promise to consecrate $5,000,000 to the treasury of the Lord.

READING OF THE REPORT.

The Secretary of the Committee, the Rev. F. F. Ellinwood, D.D., of New York, presented the report. It is as follows:—

REPORT OF THE PRESBYTERIAN MEMORIAL COMMITTEE, MAY, 1871.

The Committee appointed to raise and disburse the *Five Million Memorial Fund* was organized at 47 Exchange Place, New York, June 17, 1870, the Chairman, Winthrop S. Gilman, presiding. It was resolved that Hon. Wm. E. Dodge be requested to continue the office of Treasurer, and Rev. F. F. Ellinwood was appointed Corresponding Secretary for one year, for the general supervision of the work. Steps were immediately taken to lay before the churches a distinct plan for subscribing, collecting, reporting, and remitting their offerings according to the direction of the Assembly.

The Committee learned that during the interval between the passage of the original resolution at Pittsburgh and the final ratification at Philadelphia, only about $1,900 had been contributed to the Central Treasury, though beginnings had been made in various forms of home work among the churches.

The greater part of the $5,000,000 was yet to be raised, and eleven months remained for the work.

The small amount which had thus far been contributed, the wide differences of opinion in the Church as to the uses which should be made of the fund, and the general demand that the people should be allowed to judge of the wisdom and necessity of their own disbursements, rendered it plain that success could be attained only by adopting a policy as liberal as the instructions of the Assembly would permit.

The great object in view, as the Committee conceived it, was to render memorable the Presbyterian Reunion by an enlargement and strengthening of all the structural interests of the Church as a permanent token of gratitude to God.

The motive of highest utility must be coupled with that of commemoration.

Even aside from the question of what was feasible and what was not,—of what might succeed and what would inevitably fail,—it seemed more important to secure the greatest possible advancement of the kingdom of Christ than to present imposing results before men. Evidently no committee could realize so large an amount as five millions of dollars without seeking the co-operation and subsidizing the manifold interests of the whole Church. Each Synod and each Presbytery must take up its own work; every institution of learning must stimulate the exertions of its alumni and its local friends, and every feeble congregation must seize the opportunity both of quickening its own efforts and of gaining help from others. The Committee have, therefore, from the first, endeavored to provoke the diligence of the churches in those forms of work, within the prescribed classes, which in their judgment should present the strongest claim to their liberality. They have, however, urged particularly the *general* objects named by the Assembly, and have invariably presented the highest and most spiritual motives. As far as possible the Committee have been personally represented in the various Synods and in union meetings of the churches in the larger towns. In order to secure the more thorough co-operation of the West and Northwest, Rev. A. G. Ruliffson was, on the 1st of August, appointed Western Secretary for the remainder of the fiscal year; and the Committee have had abundant reason to rejoice in the results of that appointment.

In regard to the range of objects contemplated in this work, the brief outline recommended by the former *Committee of Ten*, and adopted by the last Assembly, has proved to be eminently wise, both in its comprehensiveness and in its limitations. It confined the effort to the main departments of structural and permanent interests, and yet forbore to enter into details which could not have been judiciously imposed beforehand, and which could only have exerted a discouraging and repressive influence. The structural objects which were indicated by the Assembly, were of five classes, viz.: Churches, Manses, Literary and Theological Institutions at Home and Abroad, Hospitals connected with the Church, and Houses for the Use of the Boards.

What proportion of the aggregate fund should be allotted to each of these classes the Assembly did not state; nor has the Committee felt authorized to decide. If one class has been found to absorb too much, and another has received too little, it is but an inevitable result of that discretionary freedom which the plan necessarily involved. To these permanent objects, as distinguished from all current work, the Committee have endeavored to confine the effort, allowing only such expansions as were conceived to exist in the spirit of this movement as first proposed. If in the practical exigencies of so many churches, seeming changes have appeared in the plan, they have been only those of natural and necessary development, as the bulb is transformed to a rooted plant.

Thus the principle which admits a complete institution must be so ramified as to cover all its parts. If the friends of a particular college, variously offer endowments, new buildings, scholarships, libraries, repairs, cancelled mortages, and grants of land, they must, of logical necessity, be included, though in the outset no such variety had occurred to any mind. So of churches, if one congregation find acceptance for a new sanctuary complete in all its parts and appurtenances, no principle of justice can exclude the poorer flock who can only offer a part of a church, as an enlargement, or a new roof, or an organ, or a bell, or even a horse-shed or a fence.

It is true, that by such a rule some humble objects are included; but He who, in the construction of his ancient sanctuary, invited even such offerings as a ram's skin or a little goat's hair, does not despise an humble gift. It is a beautiful feature of our common Memorial, that it has harmoniously combined the efforts of the wealthy and the poor. The affluent have given their tens of thousands, and with equal acceptance the toiling needlewoman has offered joyfully her mite; the merchant prince has drawn his check, and the converted Indian on the frontier has given his honest score of days' work upon the walls of God's house.

It is inevitable that the general principles governing so great an undertaking should sometimes be abused. How could it be otherwise, when so much of worldly motive mingles with all the benevolence and all the services of the Church. The Memorial work has doubtless been marred by as many exhibitions of a selfish spirit as appear in other things; but the degree of selfishness has not always been measured by mere locality, nor by the kind of Memorial object chosen. Hundreds of the noblest instances of self-sacrifice have been shown in humble congregations, which were struggling to secure a sanctuary for themselves and their neighbors about them. A voluminous record might be given of incidents and illustrations of the most touching character, and affording ample proof that many have found the Memorial work a precious means of grace.

While pursuing a liberal policy in admitting the gifts of the churches, the Committee have confined their own direct disbursements to objects of a general character, and those of the most pressing need. They have had no desire to secure any large proportion of the fund to the general treasury, except as enabling them to meet this class of wants. They would gladly have accomplished more in this respect than they have.

At a time when very general apprehension existed lest the Memorial should seriously embarrass the Church Boards, many persons in various parts of the Church expressed a desire to devote their Memorial offerings as special donations for the relief of the Boards. As such gifts found no sanction in either the letter or the spirit of the Assembly's instructions, the Committee felt that they had no authority in the premises, but they finally resolved to admit these special offerings in a separate class, subject to the action of this Assembly.

In the midst of the apprehensions just referred to, the Committee have maintained a hopeful spirit. They have so constantly received assurances that the churches which were doing most for the Memorial were even increasing their gifts to the Boards, that they have felt confident that the end of the year would show very slight deficits in our regular benevolences, if any at all. And it is with rare satisfaction and gratitude that they now find that confidence fully justified.

Comparing the reports of the Boards just rendered to this Assembly with those presented a year ago, and confining the estimate to the actual gifts of churches and individuals, as distinguished from legacies and other casual resources, they find the receipts of the United Boards, compared with the aggregates of the Separate Boards of the two branches last year, to present the following gains as compared with last year:—

Home Missions, gain over last year, $16,297.25; Church Erection, gain about $20,000; Education, deficit, $964; Publication, deficit, $9,888; Freedmen, gain about $500; Ministerial Relief, gain, $13,687.27; Foreign Missions, gain, $37,-296.89; Aggregate gain of all the Boards, $76,502.89.

It should be stated that the gains in the Foreign Board are mainly due to the accession of churches formerly contributing to the American Board of Foreign Missions; but it should also be said that there are still considerable amounts in the Memorial Treasury for the Presbyterian Board not included in their report.

There are furthermore some differences in the time of closing the fiscal year of the Boards, as compared with the previous year, but these differences, together with the fact that the Memorial report closes latest of all, will, on the whole, rather strengthen the exhibit which is here made, and will fully establish the important fact, that *during the Memorial year churches and individuals have given a larger aggregate to the Boards than in any previous year of our whole history.*

It may be proper also to dwell for a moment upon the direct benefit which the Memorial has conferred upon the various causes which the Boards represent.

On the Foreign Mission field, permanent institutions have been provided for to the amount of nearly a hundred thousand dollars.

In Church Erection on the Home field a careful estimate shows that about six hundred churches and chapels have been reared during the year and a half, of which only twenty-one have reported a cost of over $25,000. About three hundred of these, including mission chapels, have directly or indirectly received aid from the Memorial Fund. The amount which has actually been received into the treasury for this purpose is $96,282.93.

The cause of Publication has only been benefited in the enlargement of the Publishing House to the extent of about $45,300.

For the Freedmen's cause less has been done than was desirable—only about $10,000 having been reported for schools and churches devoted to their interests.

The cause of Ministerial Relief, aside from special gifts already estimated in its own reports, has received some small amounts for a permanent fund.

How far the cause of Education has been advanced may be judged by the fact that the Church has added nearly a million and a half of dollars to her educational apparatus in various permanent forms.

The relation of the Memorial effort to Home Missions is less direct, but none the less important. The recent report of the Home Mission Board shows that the churches under its care have raised $228,627 for the payment of church debts. This amount, at the safe rate of eight per cent. interest, shows a saving to the Mission Churches, and virtually to the Mission Board, of $18,130 per annum. But the whole amount of Memorial contributions reported from Home Mission churches is $339,410, and when we add the large sums given them by others for churches, manses, and repairs, we shall have an aggregate increase of not less than half a million of church property in the Home Mission field,—the effect of which will raise many churches at once, or very soon, to a position of efficiency and self-support. And, finally, the Memorial effort in all our churches, rich and poor, by removing obstacles and enlarging foundations and quickening exertion, has prepared the way for the *future* work of the various Boards beyond anything in the history of the past.

The Committee are led to believe that not the least of the

good results of this effort has been its rallying and uniting influence upon the denomination. It seems providential that the reunion should have been followed by a common and enthusiastic movement, overrunning and obliterating all the old lines of separation.

It has, moreover, strengthened our courage by the development of important principles. It has shown that there is a responsive loyalty among us, to the projects and behests of the Assembly; it has demonstrated the important fact that we are a thoroughly organized body, and that by our Presbyterian polity even so great a mass may be marshalled and wielded in the great work of Christian conquest. Nor can it be doubted that the experiment of this Memorial year has *permanently* enlarged the scale of benevolence among us. Whatever may be said of the use which the churches have made of their gifts, the great and notable fact is, that such vast amounts of money have been given at all for religious purposes, and given mainly with a sincere desire to accomplish the highest good. It is not a light thing, that in this worldly age, and amid the business discouragements which have marked the year, and with the current expenditures of all the churches still continued, and with seven regular boards to be maintained in full operation, so many extra millions of dollars should have been contributed for the permanent interests of Christ's kingdom. The fact itself is the best possible monument of reunion. The spectacle of such a movement is full of encouragement and hope.

And lest it should be said by any that these are not extra amounts; but that we have only recorded the average structural work of average years, the Committee have been at some pains to learn what has been done outside of the Memorial reckoning; and they find that by the common impulse, which, even under protest, could not wholly be resisted, more than two millions of dollars, not included in this report, has been raised during the Memorial period for the same kinds of work. There is abundant proof that the five millions which it was resolved to raise, may be set down as a clear gain above all previous years of our history as a Church. The Committee are free to confess that even their highest hopes have been more than realized in this respect. And when they contrast the discouragements that hung over their early efforts, with the general response that has at length been given, they are impressed with the fact that the result is due not to skilful management, nor to faithful labors, nor to any human influence, but to the special power of the Spirit of God moving so many hearts in all parts of the land to a common effort.

It is due to some of the best men in the Church, who from

the first have doubted the policy of such a movement, to say that they have nevertheless, in other ways, helped forward the cause of Christ in proportionate degrees. It is partly owing to the special efforts of such that the Boards have been so well sustained. The Committee rejoice in their labors also, nay, and will rejoice since every way God is glorified.

In reviewing the labors of the year the Committee take much pleasure in acknowledging the great assistance afforded them by the weekly religious press of the denomination. Perhaps never before has the power of the religious press in promoting great Church enterprises been so fully illustrated. To human view it is difficult to see how, without this valuable agency, the work of the Committee could have been accomplished. To *The Evangelist*, *The Presbyterian*, *The Interior*, *The Observer*, *The Herald and Presbyter*, *The Banner*, and *The Occident*, the thanks not only of the Committee but of the whole Church are due for their efficient aid. The Committee would also make grateful mention of the fact that furnished offices have been placed at their disposal during the year by Phelps, Dodge & Co., and that similar courtesies were tendered them by Brown Brothers & Co., and others in New York.

In presenting the actual statistics of the work, it should be premised that, owing to the tardiness of the returns from many churches, our report is necessarily incomplete. Much work known to have been accomplished is too late for this presentation. Some of the returns also have been so indistinct that a satisfactory comparison of college reports with those of churches, with a view to avoiding repetition, has been wellnigh impossible. And as the Committee have preferred to err on the safe side, they have in all cases of uncertainty ruled out college reports, though fully persuaded that by this means $200,000 is excluded from their footings.* Owing to the same difficulty no account has been made of the reports of special Memorial gifts returned by the Boards, and by the Woman's Societies. Large sums, also, gathered from individuals for churches in the West, have been excluded on account of uncertainty, though it is believed that many of them have not been reported by donors. It was the first intention of the Committee to report individual donors in some cases by name; but the difficulty of a proper discrimination has been found to be so great that such names are simply entered on the Memorial Records, while to the public they are reported in the aggregate, under a general miscellaneous head.

The classification of money received and reported thus far is as follows:—For New Church Buildings, $3,236,475.61;

*Some of these have been included in the final footings given August 1st.

Manses, $683,884.05; Repairs and Enlargement, $733,707.60; Payment of Debts, $1,083,478.72; Institutions of Learning, $1,405,548.66; Permanent Institutions in Foreign lands, $93,-509.96; Special Gifts to the Boards, $60,340.40; Hospitals, $48,665.35; Relief Fund and Sustentation, $41,150.46; Presbyterian Houses, $46,882.37; Amounts not specified by the Churches reporting it, $162,681.10; Expenses of the Committee, $11,175.63. It is with profound gratitude to God that the Committee announce as the total amount reported up to 12 o'clock to-day, SEVEN MILLIONS SIX HUNDRED AND SEVEN THOUSAND FOUR HUNDRED AND NINETY-NINE DOLLARS AND NINETY-ONE CENTS.*

Dr. Ellinwood said in the course of reading the report:

And here I wish to say personally one word which I am sure our beloved and honored Chairman would never have permitted me to embody in this report. I want the Assembly and the Presbyterian Church to know how far we have been indebted for the success of this work to the faithful labors of Winthrop S. Gilman. (Applause.) Even at the risk of intruding upon feelings, the delicacy of which I well know, I should not feel that I was doing justice to myself, or to what I regard as demanded in the case, if I did not state that nearly through the whole year he has labored side by side with me in duties properly belonging to the secretaryship. I feel that the Church has a sort of common right in such examples, and that they ought to be set on a candlestick, that others seeing them may glorify our Father who is in Heaven. (Applause.)

Upon the conclusion of the reading of the Report, a hymn of praise arose from all the assembly in the building spontaneously: "Praise God, from whom all blessings flow."

The Moderator then called upon the Rev. Dr. John Hall, of New York, to lead the Assembly in prayer. There were few whose faces did not bear the traces of the deepest emotion, while all stood as thanks were returned to Heaven.

PRAYER BY DR. JOHN HALL.

Our Father who art in Heaven, the God and Father of our Lord Jesus Christ, and God of our fathers! We have trusted

* *Full amount reported August 1st*, 1871:—Churches, $3,342,952.11; Manses, $691,709.45; Repairs, &c., $746,209.65; Payment of Debts, $1,108,933.91; Institutions of Learning, $1,460,619.84; Permanent Institutions in Foreign Lands, $94,619.98; Special Gifts to the Boards, $62,780.40; Hospitals, $49,665.35; Relief Fund and Sustentation, $44,044.21; Presbyterian Houses, $46,882.37; Amounts not designated, $172,158.60; Expenses of the Committee, $13,407.98; Total, $7,833,983.85.

in Thee, and Thou hast not suffered us to be confounded. Many a time we have come to Thee with trembling lips and with fainting hearts to offer petitions and supplications with strong crying; and now, O God, we come to Thee with joyful thanksgiving and hearty praises that we may bless and magnify Thy holy Name, and adore Thee together as a God that is faithful and that keepeth covenant, and that doth not let one word fall to the ground of all that He hath spoken unto his people. Thou art our God, and we will praise Thee. Thou art our fathers' God, and we will magnify Thy holy Name. O God, we bless Thee for what Thou hast done for us as a Church. Thou hast wrought all these works for us, Thou hast poured out upon us Thy Spirit. Thou hast helped us to gain this victory over selfishness; and we bless Thee and praise Thy holy and adorable Name. O Lord, we acknowledge before Thee that Thou givest us the power to get wealth, and Thou dost work within us to will and to do of Thy good pleasure.

For Thy mercy in bringing us together; for the joy of our happy reunion; for the inspiration in our hearts leading us to enter upon this undertaking, we bless Thee and praise Thee together here to-day.

And now we thank Thee, Heavenly Father, that what was conceived in hope and in gratitude has, through Thy great goodness and mercy, been realized so richly in the midst of us to-day. For surely Thou hast done for us exceeding abundantly above all that we hope or expected at Thy hand; and so we bless Thee. Again we raise our Ebenezer together, again we say before Thee and before the world: "Hitherto hath the Lord helped us."

God Almighty, we thank Thee for the grace given to our brethren who have been engaged in collecting these our offerings; we bless Thee for the patience, the wisdom, the diligence, the zeal, and the prayerfulness with which they have been enabled to prosecute this work; and now we pray on their behalf that there may come back abundant blessing into their souls.

We beseech Thee, Lord, strengthen them and help them for yet greater services in the cause of our precious Master. We implore Thy blessing upon all the agencies, and all the institutions that are to be strengthened, or that have been strengthened already through this Memorial work; we pray that those who are engaged in conducting them may be baptized with the Holy Ghost. God Almighty, we supplicate Thy blessing upon all the friends, our beloved brethren, who have contributed to this Memorial Fund. Lord, bless the rich. Save them from trusting in uncertain riches; and, Lord, bless the poor who have given of their poverty. May there come into their own souls seven-fold blessing. Give them a renewed sense of Thy favor, and the abiding spirit of adoption within them; and, O God, give them grace we beseech Thee, give to all our brethren who have been engaged in this work, grace to maintain that standard of Christian liberality to which in Thy goodness and mercy Thou hast raised us during this year.

And now, O God, upon our beloved Church—the Church for which Thou hast brought us, to labor and to pray—we supplicate Thy divine blessing. O Lord, save her from trusting in material resources. O Lord, keep her from entering into her work in the spirit of a secular corporation. O Lord Jesus, our King and Head, fill us with Thy Spirit, and enable us to do Thy work in the way that Thou dost approve, through the means of Thy Truth, and to the glory of Thy Name. And when, as this day, Thou dost enable us to look upon anything as completed, Lord Jesus, save us from the folly and the sin of arrogating the credit to ourselves, and help us to bring our tribute of homage and thanksgiving by laying it at Thy feet, and saying: To Thee, not unto us, O Lord, not unto us, but to Thy Name be the glory.

And now, as ministers and as elders; as the members of this General Assembly, Moderator, and members, we do together afresh consecrate and dedicate ourselves unto Thee, Father—our Father—that we may be guided, and directed, and kept by Thee continually—that we may live to the glory of that Saviour by whose redeeming work we have been saved, and that we may strive and toil forward in the power of that gracious and Divine Spirit who has come upon us in some measure, and who has strengthened us to do that over which we rejoice to-day. So may we be helped in life and in death, in our hearts and in our homes, in our pulpits and among our people, in our Presbyteries and in our Assemblies may we be helped to give glory to the Father, and to the Son, and to the Holy Ghost.

Almighty God, we supplicate Thy blessing upon all sections of our Church and upon every department of the Christian work, both at home and abroad. Pour out Thy Spirit upon our seminaries; baptize our professors and instructors of the young with the Spirit of grace and wisdom. Oh! make us, we beseech Thee, as a Church a mighty spiritual power over this whole land! And we supplicate Thee for the country at large. Surely Thou hast blessed us richly, and laid us under great responsibility. Unto us Thou hast given a good land and a large, whose mountains are iron and out of whose hills we may dig brass; Thou hast clothed our pastures with flocks, and our valleys with corn; Thou hast given to the people abundance of bread, and Thou hast raised us and strengthened us and kept us as a nation, and hast lifted us to a high place among the nations of the earth.

For this we praise Thee. And, O God, we pray that this, our beloved Church, the Church of our fathers, may be the happy and honored instrument, in Thy hand, of blessing this entire nation; of purifying the public sentiment; of enlightening the public darkness; of guiding national influences; so that, ourselves in peace and in righteousness, we may be made an unspeakable blessing among all the nations of the earth. O Lord, continue among us, as a Church, this sweet brotherly love. O Lord, give us more and more of the spirit of forbearance, the spirit of magnanimity, the spirit of mutual confidence and cheerful trustfulness. O Lord, make us strong in common sympathies, common aims, common desires. O Lord, make us strong through the indwelling of the Divine Spirit; let the power of Christ continue to rest upon us. Receive our thanksgivings, pardon our sins. Lord, forgive the sins of our lives; and when any merely human motive has entered into the performance of this great and high duty, the consummation of which we witness this day, Lord, forgive the sin we beseech Thee, and accept the service and the sacrifice that Thy people bring to Thee, and in them and in their labors, be Thou, O Lord, glorified. We ask these things in the name of Jesus; that precious Name through which we present our thanksgivings and our praises. And unto the Father and the Son and the Holy Ghost, one Supreme Jehovah, be glory and homage, dominion and power, world without end, Amen.

The Rev. Dr. Eells, of Cleveland, said: It is manifest from this paper just read by the Secretary, that there are some details rendering the work of this Committee not yet complete. I move that the report we have just heard, and which has so much thrilled us to-day, be accepted and referred to a special committee of the usual number, to be appointed by the Moderator.

A committee was accordingly appointed, Dr. Eells, chairman. In due time Dr. Eells presented the following report, which was passed unanimously by a standing vote of the Assembly.

Report of the Special Committee on the Memorial Fund.

The Convention of the United Churches at Pittsburgh agreed with enthusiasm to the following resolution :—

Resolved, That it is incumbent on the Presbyterian Church in the United States of America, one in organization, one in faith, and one in effort, to make a special offering to the treasury of the Lord, of Five Millions of Dollars; and we pledge ourselves, first of all, to seek in our daily petitions the blessing of God to make this resolution effectual; and second, that we will, with untiring perseverance and personal effort, endeavor to animate the whole Church with the purpose to secure the accomplishment of this great work before the third Thursday of May, 1871.

The Joint Committee reported this resolution to the General Assembly at Philadelphia, and recommended that a committee be appointed to raise and disburse this Memorial Fund, the contributions to be limited to the objects specified in their further report. This recommendation was adopted, and the committee was appointed, whose report of a year's service has so thrilled this Assembly and the whole Church—the further consideration of which was referred to this Committee. The details of their work as respects responsibility, devotion, energy, and patient toil, can be known only to the honored brethren whose names will for ever be identified with the result. The result itself is grand, perhaps without parallel—viz., that $7,607,499.91 were contributed to the Fund during the year, besides more than $2,000,000 which were given for objects that might properly be included within the list adopted, but which, because of the choice of the donors, or for reasons growing out of the strict construction of their rules, the Committee did not feel at liberty to include in the Fund; and at least $200,000 given to various educational institutions, which were not reckoned, lest the amounts composing this sum might possibly have been reported by the churches, and thus be duplicated, though this was not likely;—making a total of what the Church has really given during the year to be $9,807,499.91—or, in round numbers, which will hardly be below the truth, $10,000,000. A notable fact connected with this Memorial gift, moreover, should be ever borne in mind—viz., that it is not laid on the altar at the sacrifice of the regular benevolent work of the Church, but in addition to contributions to our Boards, in the aggregate "greater than in any previous year of our history."

Such is the condensed record of a work, among the most remarkable, all things considered, of all that are mentioned in the annals of the Church. Your Committee will not be expected to present again in detail the items and facts of the admirable report given into their hands. Yet there are some inferences from these, and some considerations respecting them, which they commend to the attention of the Assembly.

1. It is manifest that the great success of this effort has been largely dependent on the wisdom and efficiency, and Christian spirit of the gentlemen who formed the "Memorial Fund Committee." It is difficult to conceive the magnitude, and in some

phases of it, the perplexity of the attempt to obtain and wisely distribute $5,000,000 on such conditions as were imposed upon this Committee. That it should have been done at all is a marvel. That it should have been done with such rare ability, and satisfaction of the Church, and manifest approbation of her Head, may well excite our gratitude and praise.

2. This great success leaves no doubt that there is among our members a degree of love to Christ, and love for our Church; a willingness on the part of the rich to give of their abundance, and on the part of the poor a desire to give through their self-denial towards the complete equipment of Zion in all her departments for the service of her Lord, and for the salvation of men, which may be trusted in any future emergencies, or when there is urgent necessity for advance. We have been too ready, perhaps, to say that Presbyterians have little zeal for the vigorous progress of their own denomination. We have been expected to aid in the support of union and voluntary agencies for the spread of the Gospel, and the redemption of the world. Nor should we wish to be hereafter unworthy of the honor on this account which others have been free to render. But we have not been known to have such "*esprit de corps*," such reliable and self-sacrificing, and general, sanctified self-love and regard for our distinctive organic peculiarities as is now most clearly demonstrated. We have known—the world has had proof—that Presbyterians love Christ, love Christians of every name, love the common cause in which all Christians should ever take an abiding interest. Hereafter, while we would love neither Christ nor Christians of every name, nor our common cause any less, but even more, we can point to the history of this glorious year for proof that Presbyterians love intensely, enthusiastically, and, because of its vital connection with the glory of Christ and the success of His kingdom, the Presbyterian Church. We can make this fact the basis for more extended and permanent agencies for evangelization. We can make it a new point of departure, as respects our whole future career. We can trust our people respecting the sublime mission we believe our denomination should accept, in the current religious history of our nation and the world.

3. As intelligent preparation for great efficiency implies the purpose to attempt it, we may assume that the Church intends to enter upon the broader work, for which both the spirit she has manifested and the effort she has made have prepared her; and her leaders may be bold in their plans for progress if they are prudent and wise. Pastors and elders in our separate churches—Presbyterians within their bounds—our Boards, in in prosecuting the more general work of the denomination, may

take this marvellous exhibition, which will grow upon us as we contemplate it, as their warrant for the hearty co-operation of our members, of all classes, in any carefully digested schemes for extension and doing the Master's will. There is great promise of growth, and consequent usefulness, in this outpouring of money. It has taught the people that, with the blessing of God, it is easy to do great things; that even improbable things may be achieved by the Church; that liberality is itself a blessing. It has taught them that the poor are of importance, even in money-giving, as well as the rich. It has cultivated a more general interest in the benevolent work of the Church, because a much larger number have stock in the means by which it is to be promoted. Prayer is more earnest, intelligence is more universal, the ear of the whole number is more sensitive to appeals, and while recklessness and zeal without knowledge will result as ever before, true forecast and prudent calls for advance will meet cheering and eager response. Your Committee feel that this is the marked and special lesson of this success. It is the clear summons of our Lord, through the Church, to those who are her leaders, that they be men prepared for the events with which Providence is burdened. It is the assurance He vouchsafes, that whatever piety requires for the prosecution of its ends, it shall not be withheld.

4. Although a large portion of our churches have contributed to the Fund, and the Committee have been persistent in their efforts to induce all to have a share in the gift, there are some that have neglected the opportunity, and some that have been obliged to postpone action till it was too late, according to the provision of the resolution that the books be closed on the third Thursday of May. For every reason it is desirable that these churches be permitted to place themselves on the roll, while it is also important that the date first proposed be the end of the proper work the Committee had in hand. This may be done by the publication of a supplemental list of churches, to include all that may send their reports before a certain fixed date of the coming year, the churches designating, as before, the objects to which they wish their contributions to be applied. It is suggested for such churches that, so far as possible, they bestow their gifts for the special benefit of the regular agencies of the Church, as such gifts are to be added to the Memorial Fund by the direction of this General Assembly.

5. The figures of the Memorial Committee are to be relied upon as correct in all their particulars. But it is to be regretted that there has been no uniform rule adopted by the Presbyteries respecting their report of the sums given to different

objects. Some report Memorial offerings also in the columns of their statistical tables, and others make no such report So that these tables cannot be a fair exhibit of what has been done during the year for the several departments of Church advance. Your Committee are not able to suggest any practicable remedy for this misfortune, and therefore are content with this mere reference to it. For reliable particulars concerning the distribution of the Memorial offerings, we must examine the detailed report, and list of churches, to be published by the Committee.

Having alluded to these inferences and considerations, among the many that might be presented, we conclude our report by recommending that the Assembly adopt the following resolutions:—

1. That we devoutly thank Almighty God, of whom come both riches and honor, and who also can give strength unto all, so that they may be able to offer willingly after this sort, that He has inclined our people to lay this Memorial gift upon His altar.

2. That we thank our brethren who have served the Church on the Committee—the most satisfactory results of whose wisdom and patience and work is given us in this report—for their fidelity and devotion in the discharge of this sacred yet difficult duty to which they were called, while we feel that this result must be their most worthy reward.

3. That we congratulate the Church upon such proof of what she is able to achieve, and of her more complete equipment for the future, upon the broad threshold of which our reunion has placed her, with the promise of great success; and that the contribution of so large a sum of money, in addition to the support of the regular agencies of the Church, leaves no doubt that she can hereafter answer any demands which the increased and more active piety of her members may make upon her wealth.

4. That while there is evident need of even more money, especially for the relief of our new churches—six hundred of which are believed to be still without houses of worship—and for the greater success of our home and foreign missionary work; and while we believe the Church is willing to respond to this necessity, the raising of this money may now be accomplished by the Boards of the Church, and the continuance of any special agencies for this purpose will not be wise.

5. That we accept this report of the Committee as evidence of their completed work, yet that the Committee be continued till the session of the next General Assembly, that they may superintend the details that may still require their attention, and make their final report to that body.

6. That as there are some churches which, for various reasons, have been unable to make their reports, yet desire to have a place among those contributing to this Fund, the Committee be requested to delay the printing of the roll of churches and individuals so contributing, till the first of August next. That before that date any churches or individuals may have opportunity to report for regular insertion, any sums that may have been given previous to the third Thursday of May, and all others may report what they desire to be added to the Fund, their names and gifts being printed in a list that may be regarded as a supplement to the regular report.

All which is respectfully submitted.

Signed by the Committee.

JAMES EELLS, *Chairman.*

SYNOD OF ALBANY.

PRESBYTERY OF ALBANY.

Ministers.	Churches.	Home Objects.	General Objects.	Total.
H. L. Teller...............	Amsterdam, Second...	$1,000 00	$692 00	$1,692 00
J. T. Backus, D.D.........	Schenectady, First....	5,000 00	3,000 00	8,000 00
David Lyon..............	Mariaville	....	25 00	25 00
John Woodbridge, D.D....	Saratoga Springs......	5,000 00	....	5,000 00
J. McClusky Blayney......	Albany, First.........	13,178 21	406 50	13,584 71
Ebenezer Halley, D.D.....	Albany, Third........	631 00	....	631 00
Anson J. Upson, D.D......	Albany, Second	12,127 00	....	12,127 00
Henry Darling, D.D.......	Albany, Fourth........	....	19,533 27	19,533 27
Amos H. Dean............	Albany, Sixth.........	275 00	....	275 00
....	Albany, State St......	950 00	3,300 00	4,250 00
J. M. Allis......	Albany, Sprague Ch...	285 00	....	285 00
....	Gloversville..........	1,800 00	....	1,800 00
George Harkness..........	Kingsboro	4,085 55	50 00	4,135 55
....	Goodwill.............	7,500 00	....	7,500 00
Wm. H. Millham.........	Galway..............	800 00	....	800 00
David Herron............	Bethlehem...........	400 00	....	400 00
Dupuytren Vermilye.......	Hamilton Union.......	120 00	....	120 00
C. H. Baldwin............	Johnstown...........	10,000 00	....	10,000 00
Andrew Johnston.........	West Milton..........	156 00	....	156 00
John Mitchell............	West Galway..........	195 00	50 00	245 00
Wm. J. Blain.............	Amsterdam, First.....	....	23 00	23 00
....	Carlisle...............	325 00	70 00	395 00
Anson H. Seeley..........	Esperance	130 00	30 00	160 00
....	Rockwell's Falls.......	52 00	....	52 00
Geo. Craig.......	Corinth..............	25 00	52 80	77 80
....	Ballston	1,000 00	116 50	1,116 50
John M. Allis............	Batchellerville	900 00	....	900 00
R. A. Hill................	Princetown	400 00	32 00	432 00
....	Broadalbin...........	40 00	....	40 00
....	Tribes' Hill...........	300 00	....	300 00
....	Jefferson.............	150 00	....	150 00
F. S. Jewell, Ph.D.P......	Greenbush............	789 00	....	789 00
Albert C. Bishop..........	Sand Lake............	3,871 00	....	3,871 00
		$71,484 76	$27,381 07	$98,863 83

Churches not reported, 16.

—o—

PRESBYTERY OF CHAMPLAIN.

Ministers.	Churches.	Home Objects.	General Objects.	Total.
John Bradshaw...........	Mooers	$1,500 00	....	$1,500 00
Edwin A. Bulkley, D.D....	Plattsburgh...........	3,500 00	$5 00	3,505 00
H. E. Butler..............	Keeseville............	728 93	....	728 93
Charles D. Flagler........	Chateaugay...........	440 46	26 98	467 44
S. J. Abbott..............	Chazy................	140 00	10 00	150 00
Benjamin Merrill.........	Ausable Forks........	300 00	....	300 00
....	Am. Church, Montreal.	....	25 00	25 00
		$6,609 39	$66 98	$6,676 37

Churches not reported, 11.

PRESBYTERY OF COLUMBIA.

Ministers.	Churches.	Home Objects.	General Objects.	Total.
G. W. Warner	Canaan Centre	$91 00	$598 25	$689 25
Geo. O. Phelps	Valatie	500 00	....	500 00
John McVey	New Lebanon	150 00	43 21	193 21
David R. Frazer	Hudson	4,635 00	625 00	5,260 00
J. A. Clark	Spencertown, St. Peter's	295 00	39 00	334 00
Winthrop H. Phelps	Hillsdale	373 98	5 00	378 98
....	Rensselaerville	755 00	....	755 00
Charles Kendall	Ashland	450 00	25 00	475 00
....	Livingstonville	....	25 00	25 00
Charles Kendall	Windham Centre	160 00	47 00	207 00
George A. Howard, D.D.	Catskill	4,000 00	....	4,000 00
Charles Boynton	Durham, First	243 00	153 00	396 00
Byron Bosworth	Greenville	203 24	....	203 24
		$11,856 22	$1,560 46	$13,416 68

Churches not reported, 6.

—o—

PRESBYTERY OF TROY.

Ministers.	Churches.	Home Objects.	General Objects.	Total.
Lewis Kellogg	North Granville	$2,600 00	....	$2,600 00
A. J. Fennel	Glenn's Falls	....	$232 00	232 00
Marvin R. Vincent, D.D.	Troy, First	8,000 00	....	8,000 00
William Irvin	Troy, Second	135 00	2,865 00	3,000 00
....	Troy, Third	....	37 00	37 00
Chas. E. Robinson, D.D.	Troy, Second St	12,000 00	....	12,000 00
....	Troy, Woodside	5,000 00	230 00	5,230 00
....	Oakwood Ave	800 00	....	800 00
A. T. De Witt	Troy Park	900 00	700 00	1,600 00
M. C. Bronson	Chestertown	775 00	....	775 00
John Tatlock	Hoosic Falls	2,025 00	....	2,025 00
Chas. J. Hill	Whitehall, First Ch	1,300 00	112 00	1,412 00
Geo. W. Martin	Schaghticoke	210 00	....	210 00
G. P. Tyler, D.D	Lansingburgh, Olivet	2,100 00	....	2,100 00
H. Davies	Middle Granville	600 00	....	600 00
A. E. Smith	Warrensburgh	280 00	....	280 00
J. H. Noble, D.D	Johnsonville	69 80	....	69 80
C. C. Thorne	Stillwater, First	2,000 00	....	2,000 00
William M. Johnson	Cohoes	3,200 00	....	3,200 00
G. I. Taylor	Malta	....	19 00	19 00
R. P. H. Vail	Waterford	4,000 00	575 00	4,575 00
Stephen Bush	Green Island	2,000 00	....	2,000 00
J. E. Platter	Sandy Hill	1,000 00	....	1,000 00
....	Cambridge	....	23 00	23 00
		$48,994 80	$4,793 00	$53,787 80

Churches not reported, 13.

SYNOD OF ATLANTIC.

PRESBYTERY OF ATLANTIC.

Ministers.	Churches.	Home Objects.	General Objects.	Total.
S. S. Murkland...........	Freedom............	....	$10 00	$10 00
			$10 00	$10 00

Churches not reported, 14.

—o—

PRESBYTERY OF CATAWBA.

Ministers.	Churches.	Home Objects.	General Objects.	Total.
S. Mattoon, D.D..........	Charlotte.............	$200 00	....	$200 00
S. Mattoon, D.D....	Mt. Olive.............	....	$29 25	29 25
S. C. Alexander...........	Woodland.............	....	270 00	270 00
Luke Dorland.............	Concord	....	35 00	35 00
Luke Dorland.............	Poplar Tent...........	....	67 00	67 00
John C. Carson...........	Davidson's River......	....	6 00	6 00
		$200 00	$407 25	$607 25

Churches not reported, 15.

—o—

PRESBYTERY OF EAST FLORIDA.

Ministers.	Churches.	Home Objects.	General Objects.	Total.
C. O. Reynolds...........	St. Augustine.........	$3,000 00	$50 00	$3,050 00
M. L. P. Hill.............	Jacksonville	1,500 00	....	1,500 00
		$4,500 00	$50 00	$4,550 00

PRESBYTERY OF KNOX.

Ministers.	Churches.	Home Objects.	General Objects.	Total.
David Laney.............	Macon, Wash. Ave....	....	$45 00	$45 00
			$45 00	$45 00

—o—

PRESBYTERY OF YADKIN.

Ministers.	Churches.	Home Objects.	General Objects.	Total.
S. S. Murkland............	Freedom.............	$750 00	....	$750 00
Amos S. Billingsley........	Statesville	....	$55 00	55 00
W. J. Williams............	Mocksville............	800 00	....	800 00
W. J. Williams............	Mt. Zion.............	....	5 00	5 00
W. J. Williams............	Mt. Vernon...........	200 00	....	200 00
H. Baker.................	Salisbury............	....	2 40	2 40
H. Baker.................	Gold Hill............	....	3 20	3 20
James A. Chresfield.......	Lexington............	....	5 00	5 00
		$1,750 00	$70 60	$1,820 60

Churches not reported, 9.

SYNOD OF BALTIMORE.

PRESBYTERY OF BALTIMORE.

Ministers.	Churches.	Home Objects.	General Objects.	Total.
John C. Backus, D.D......	Baltimore, First.......	....	$7,407 58	$7,407 58
Jon. Edwards, D.D........	Baltimore, Second.....	....	60 00	60 00
D. C. Marquis............	Baltimore, Westminster	....	275 00	275 00
J. S. Ramsey.............	Aisquith St...........	$1,200 00	....	1,200 00
James M. Maxwell.........	Baltimore, Twelfth....	2,700 00	....	2,700 00
W. G. Hillman............	Baltimore, South......	341 00	....	341 00
S. D. Noyes..............	Baltimore, Green St...	210 58	....	210 58
Robt. H. Williams........	Frederick.............	385 00	....	385 00
I. J. Henderson, D.D.....	Annapolis	125 00	100 00	225 00
William H. Cooke.........	Havre de Grace.......	600 00	....	600 00
J. D. Fitzgerald	Cumberland, First Ch.	20 00	174 00	194 00
Isaac M. Patterson........	Emmittsburg	250 00	....	250 00
Isaac M. Patterson........	Piney Creek..........	250 00	....	250 00
A. S. Rankin	Lonaconing...........	255 00	....	255 00
Alex. S. Thorne...........	Clearspring...........	800 00	....	800 00
Isaac M. Patterson........	Taneytown	40 50	....	40 50
		$7,177 08	$8,016 58	$15,193 66

Churches not reported, 23.

—o—

PRESBYTERY OF WASHINGTON CITY.

Ministers.	Churches.	Home Objects.	General Objects.	Total.
John C. Smith, D.D......	Washington, Fourth...	....	$1,050 00	$1,050 00
Byron Sunderland, D.D...	Washington, First.....	....	326 00	326 00
B. F. Bittinger............	Washington, Seventh St	$5,500 00	....	5,500 00
John N. Coombs..........	Washington, Western..	1,000 00	....	1,000 00
John Chester.............	Wash'n, Metropolitan..	3,000 00	....	3,000 00
Samuel S. Mitchell........	Wash'n, New York Ave.	1,563 50	954 50	2,518 00
W. McAtee..............	Alexandria, First......	....	12 00	12 00
David H. Riddle, Jr......	Lewinsville and Falls..	600 00	....	600 00
Joseph E. Nourse.........	Clifton	2,500 00	....	2,500 00
Joseph E. Nourse..........	Manassas.............	1,350 00	....	1,350 00
David W. Moffat..........	Bridge St., Georgetown	900 00	1,157 00	2,057 00
....	Damestown...........	....	12 50	12 50
		$16,413 50	$3,512 00	$19,925 50

Churches not reported, 8.

PRESBYTERY OF NEW CASTLE.

Ministers.	Churches.	Home Objects.	General Objects.	Total.
....	Smyrna..............	$2,000 00	....	$2,000 00
John Patton, D.D.........	Middletown (Forest)...	1,300 00	....	1,300 00
John B. Spotswood, D.D...	New Castle...........	....	$588 00	588 00
Gaylord L. More..........	Green Hill...........	600 00	....	600 00
John Crowell, D.D........	Odessa (Drawyers).....	1,300 00	....	1,300 00
S. R. Scofield............	Delaware City.........	1,600 00	....	1,600 00
Edward Webb.............	Glassgow, (Pencader)..	....	95 00	95 00
....	Snow Hill............	550 00	50 00	600 00
H. Mathews..............	Elkton...............	3,715 00	....	3,715 00
J. L. Vallandigham.......	White Clay Creek.....	204 00	....	204 00
J. L. Vallandigham.......	Head of Christiana....	267 00	....	267 00
S. A. Gayley.............	Lower W. Nottingham	4,000 00	....	4,000 00
....	Red Clay Creek.......	3,945 09	....	3,945 09
Richard A. Mallery........	Milford..............	250 00	....	250 00
J. Garland Harnner.......	Wicomico.............	1,100 00	400 00	1,500 00
L. Marks.................	Hanover St., Wilming'n	8,000 00	....	8,000 00
R. C. Allison.............	Port Penn............	500 00	....	500 00
J. L. Polk................	Pitt's Creek...........	596 00	50 00	646 00
D. W. Moore..............	Lower Brandywine....	3,000 00	....	3,000 00
S. Murdock...............	Felton...............	60 00	....	60 00
J. H. Johns..............	Rock.................	1,000 00	....	1,000 00
J. H. Johns..............	Zion.................	200 00	10 00	210 00
Charles D. Shaw..........	Wilmington, Central...	11,436 67	10,986 79	22,423 46
S. H. McKown............	Wilmington, First.....	5,090 00	....	5,090 00
Geo. H. Smyth............	Wilmington, West.....	25,640 00	....	25,640 00
D. J. Beale...............	St. George...........	....	1,575 00	1,575 00
Charles P. Mallery.........	Chesapeake City......	606 00	82 10	688 10
....	Newark..............	2,425 00	....	2,425 00
....	Bridgeville...........	1,000 00	....	1,000 00
....	Georgetown..........	610 00	....	610 00
....	Port Deposit..........	14,000 00	....	14,000 00
		$94,994 76	$13,836 89	$108,831 65

Churches not reported, 20.

—o—

PRESBYTERY OF RIO DE JANEIRO.

Ministers.	Churches.	Home Objects.	General Objects.	Total.
A. L. Blackford...........	Rio de Janeiro........	$30 00	....	$30 00
F. G. C. Snyder...........	Sao Paulo............	30 15	....	30 15
		$60 15	....	$60 15

SYNOD OF CHINA.*

Ministers.	Churches.	Home Objects.	General Objects.	Total.
			$1,000 00	$1,000 00
			$1,000 00	$1,000 00

SYNOD OF CINCINNATI.

PRESBYTERY OF CHILLICOTHE.

Ministers.	Churches.	Home Objects.	General Objects.	Total.
W. J. McSurely...........	Hillsboro.............	$2,315 00	$100 00	$2,415 00
McK. Williamson.........	Marshall.............	137 00	....	137 00
Geo. Carpenter............	Washington..........	6,500 00	410 00	6,910 00
H. W. Biggs...............	Chillicothe, First......	1,000 00	2,265 00	3,265 00
W. H. Prestley	Chillicothe, Third.....	620 00	130 00	750 00
R. C. Galbraith, Jr........	Concord..............	203 00	10 00	213 00
S. D. Crothers.............	Greenfield, First......	1,700 00	46 00	1,746 00
Norman Jones............	North Fork...........	1,600 00	....	1,600 00
Norman Jones............	Union................	150 00	....	150 00
T. M. Stevenson..........	New Plymouth........	600 00	....	600 00
B. T. DeWitt..............	Frankfort............	525 00	....	525 00
Rob't N. Adams...........	Hamden..............	1,100 00	....	1,100 00
		$16,450 00	$2,961 00	$19,411 00

Churches not reported, 23.

* The Synod of China, which stands in alphabetical order next to the Synod of Baltimore, is represented in the common Memorial by $1,000, reported by Rev. Hunter Corbett, of the Presbytery of Shautung. The money was contributed by brethren on the field for the training school at Cheefou, but the names of individuals or churches contributing are not given.

PRESBYTERY OF DAYTON.

Ministers.	Churches.	Home Objects.	General Objects.	Total.
Thos. E. Thomas, D.D....	Dayton, First.........	$12,000 00	....	$12,000 00
J. S. Kemper	Dayton, Third........	1,935 00	$965 00	2,900 00
R. T. Drake.............	Miami City...........	1,275 00	190 00	1,465 00
John L. Gage...........	Franklin............	300 00	....	300 0(
Ellis S. Weaver...........	Clifton...............	1,475 00	116 26	1,591 26
Samuel Findley...........	New Jersey...........	575 00	355 00	930 00
Philip H. Mowry..........	Springfield, Second....	....	1,202 00	1,202 00
J. L. Russell.............	Middletown...........	4,000 00	335 00	4,335 00
J. H. Montgomery........	Xenia................	3,445 00	....	3,445 00
....	Dick's Creek..........	....	150 00	150 00
Dan'l Tenney............	Troy.................	1,200 00	109 25	1,309 25
James R. Hughes.........	East Dayton..........	1,586 07	....	1,586 07
T. M. Hopkins...........	Piqua, First.........	2,541 00	....	2,541 00
W. H. Hummins..........	Osborn..............	500 00	....	500 00
G. A. Beattie...........	New Carlisle (Honey Creek............	....	200 00 130 00	200 00 130 00
....	Dayton, Third St......	....	22,000 00	22,000 00
D. R. Colmery...........	Yellow Springs.......	300 00	....	300 00
Dan'l A. Tawney..........	Tippecanoe...........	3,525 00	....	3,525 00
J. W. Scott, D.D., LL.D...	Eaton	300 00	....	300 00
J. W. Scott, D.D., LL.D...	Camden	....	15 00	15 00
....	New Paris...........	200 00	....	200 00
Dan'l A. Tawney..........	Fletcher.............	150 00	....	150 00
Chas. H. Raymond........	Bethel...............	....	48 50	48 50
A. H. Young.............	Oxford...............	190 00	25 00	215 00
J. B. Morton.............	Venice...............	1,400 00	....	1,400 00
Sam'l M. Anderson, D.D...	Hamilton.............	4,000 00	....	4,000 00
W. S. Rogers........... ..	Harmony.............	....	57 00	57 00
....	College Corner........	....	50 00	50 00
		$40,897 07	$25,948 01	$66,845 08

Churches not reported, 21.

—o—

PRESBYTERY OF PORTSMOUTH.

Ministers.	Churches.	Home Objects.	General Objects.	Total.
Jesse H. Lockhart........	Russelville............	$5,500 00	....	$5,500 00
Irwin L. Caton...........	Georgetown..........	....	$1,000 00	1,000 00
D. E. Bierce.............	Ripley..........	8,105 25	142 00	8,247 00
John E. Carson..........	Red Oak.............	140 00	182 95	322 95
E. P. Pratt, D.D..........	Portsmouth	7,438 00	833 00	8,271 00
A. A. Jimeson............	Hanging Rock........	2,141 50	....	2,141 50
E. P. Adams.............	Sandy Spring.........	1,400 00	....	1,400 00
E. P. Adams.............	Rome...............	89 00	....	89 00
H. Calhoun..............	Ironton..............	3,000 00	62 00	3,062 00
....	Jackson..............	150 00	....	150 00
....	Madison	....	30 00	30 00
John Heckmann........ ..	Portsmouth, First Ger.	600 00	....	600 00
Walter Mitchell........ ..	Gallipolis............	707 50	....	707 50
J. R. Gibson.............	Eckmansville	110 00	10 00	120 00
		$29,381 25	$2,259 95	$31,641 20

Churches not reported, 15.

PRESBYTERY OF CINCINNATI.

Ministers.	Churches.	Home Objects.	General Objects.	Total.
John Lichtenstein.........	Cincinnati, Ger. First.	$1,500 00	....	$1,500 00
G. W. Winners............	Cincinnati, Ger. Second	1,087 00	....	1,087 00
Charles L. Thompson......	Cincinnati, First......	....	$1,325 00	1,325 00
....	Cincinnati, Second....	....	4,035 00	4,035 00
C. H. Taylor, D.D.........	Cincinnati, Third.....	....	10,420 00	10,420 00
A. B. Morey.............	Cincinnati, Fifth......	793 36	2,092 50	2,885 86
....	Cincinnati, Sixth......	....	20 41	20 41
Fred. W. Brauns..........	Cincinnati, Seventh...	1,733 00	778 36	2,511 36
O. A. Hills..............	Cincinnati, Central....	5,570 00	500 00	6,070 00
W. C. McCune............	Cincinnati, Lincoln P'k	1,066 00	....	1,066 00
A. A. E. Taylor..........	Cincinnati, Mt. Auburn	5,900 00	2,500 00	8,400 00
M. A. Hoge, D.D..........	Cincinnati, W't H's, 1st	819 30	4,350 00	5,169 30
Geo. H. Fullerton.........	Cincinnati, Lane Sem'y	400 00	4,668 00	5,068 00
H. A. Ketchum...........	New Richmond.......	1,600 00	....	1,600 00
....	Bantam	18 00	20 00	38 00
James Black.............	Moscow...............	....	5 00	5 00
....	Sharonville...........	....	50 00	50 00
....	Pleasant Ridge........	8,386 00	....	8,386 00
....	Lockland and Reading	483 25	62 50	545 75
....	Madisonville..........	....	20 00	20 00
J. B. Foster.............	Cumminsville.........	1,295 00	....	1,295 00
Thos. F. Cortelyou........	Montgomery..........	....	86 00	86 00
" "	Somerset.............	315 00	....	315 00
H. A. Rossiter...........	Loveland.............	300 00	....	300 00
I. J. Cushman...........	Bethel................	3,130 00	285 00	3,415 00
....	Williamsburg.........	....	9 25	9 25
W. B. Spence............	Pleasant Run.........	100 00	....	100 00
J. Haight................	Lebanon, First Ch.....	1,452 00	375 00	1,827 00
Wm. H. Janus............	Springdale...........	2,042 00	....	2,042 00
W. J. McKnight, D.D.....	Avondale............	3,515 00	....	3,515 00
....	Mt. Carmel..........	....	15 00	15 00
....	Elizabeth and Berea...	....	103 00	103 00
W. A. Bosworth..........	College Hill..........	375 00	818 00	1,193 00
....	Delhi................	250 00	....	250 00
....	Cleves...............	....	15 50	15 50
....	Mt. Pleasant..........	1,800 00	....	1,800 00
		$43,929 91	$32,553 52	$76,483 43

Churches not reported, 13.

SYNOD OF CLEVELAND.

PRESBYTERY OF STEUBENVILLE.

Ministers.	Churches.	Home Objects.	General Objects.	Total.
John Arthurs	Oak Ridge	$300 00	224 00	$524 00
Alex. Swaney, D.D	New Hagerstown	100 00	317 00	417 00
T. A. McCurdy	Steubenville, First	55,000 00	355 00	55,355 00
O. R. Campbell	Steubenville, Second	39,000 00	1,900 00	40,900 00
Geo. Soul	German Ch., Steuben'le	250 00		250 00
Robt. Herron	Ridge	200 00	112 60	312 60
M. A. Parkinson	Bloomfield		2,195 00	2,195 00
Israel Price	Annapolis		250 00	250 00
" "	Richmond	100 00		100 00
W. R. Vincent	Island Creek	2,088 00	1,052 00	3,140 00
J. H. Blackford	Beech Springs	520 00	1,175 00	1,695 00
Samuel Patterson	Feed Springs	450 00		450 00
	Amsterdam	200 00		200 00
T. V. Milligan	Waynesburgh	992 00	416 00	1,408 00
" "	Bethlehem	400 00	280 50	680 50
Jos. Patterson	New Cumberland		35 00	35 00
" "	Cannonsburgh	2,000 00		2,000 00
	Uricksville			
J. F. Boyd	Cross Creek	356 75	70 00	426 75
" "	Pleasant Hill		225 00	225 00
	Center(New Alexander)	65 00		65 00
W. R. Kirkwood	Smithfield	814 00		814 00
	Two Ridges(Winters'le)	1,176 00		1,176 00
	New Philadelphia	375 00		375 00
C. W. Wyckoff	East Springfield	475 00	85 00	560 00
	Bacon Ridge	405 00	245 00	650 00
	Minerva	500 00	770 00	1,270 00
	Still Fork	325 00	200 00	525 00
Cyrus J. Hunter	Dennison	16,000 00		16,000 00
Robert Hays	Bethel	111 00	40 00	151 00
" "	Salineville	112 75	10 00	122 75
J. Swan	Yellow Creek		785 00	785 00
Wm. Dalzell	Madison		85 00	85 00
Geo. W. Riggle	East Liverpool	1,112 00		1,112 00
	Irondale	2,058 00		2,058 00
Samuel L. Dickey	Kilgore		55 00	55 00
J. Simpson	Monroeville	75 00		75 00
	Wellsville	13,000 00		13,000 00
	Longs Run	1,650 00		1,650 00
	Carrolton	400 00		400 00
J. O. E. Simpson	Corinth	1,300 00	50 00	1,350 00
		$141,910 50	$10,932 10	$152,842 60

Churches not reported, 11.

PRESBYTERY OF MAHONING.

Ministers.	Churches.	Home Objects.	General Objects.	Total.
Robt. Dickson, D.D.......	New Lisbon..........	$2,050 00	....	$2,(50 00
H. B. Eldred............	Kinsman.............	116 00	$679 00	795 00
N. S. Bailey............	Warren..............	35,000 00	....	35,000 00
B. F. Sharp.............	Ellsworth...........	375 00	565 00	940 00
D. H. Evans.............	Youngstown..........	13,270 85	30 00	13,300 85
H. B. Fry...............	Salem...............	2,375 00	360 00	2,735 00
J. S. Grimes............	Alliance............	2,000 00	....	2,000 00
W. Dickson..............	Deerfield...........	880 00	320 00	1,200 00
" "	Beloit..............	100 00	....	100 00
Jas. P. Irwin...........	Canfield............	693 00	....	693 00
....	Middle Sandy........	....	78 00	78 00
A. B. Maxwell, S.S......	Leetonia............	5,000 00	....	5,000 00
....	Newton..............	....	58 12	58 12
....	Farmington..........	1,028 00	....	1,028 00
S. D. Taylor............	Newton Falls........	200 00	....	200 00
....	Gustavus............	....	10 00	10 00
Dan'l Williams..........	Mineral Ridge.......	1,370 00	....	1,370 00
R. L. Williams..........	Massillon...........	700 00	....	700 00
E. Buckingham, D.D......	Canton..............	2,750 00	....	2,750 00
		$67,807 85	$2,100 12	$69,907 97

Churches not reported, 17.

---o---

PRESBYTERY OF ST. CLAIRSVILLE.

Ministers.	Churches.	Home Objects.	General Objects.	Total.
....	Mount Pleasant......	....	$188 38	$188 38
T. R. Crawford, D.D.....	Nottingham..........	$150 00	63 00	213 00
W. M. Grimes, D.D.......	Cadiz...............	8,000 00	....	8,000 00
H. W. Parks.............	Short Creek.........	95 00	85 75	180 75
A. Armstrong............	Wheeling Valley.....	....	30 00	30 00
H. W. Parks.............	Little York.........	....	15 00	15 00
R. Tannehill............	Birmingham..........	....	35 00	35 00
Geo. McDonald,..........	Bellsville..........	....	45 00	45 00
" "	Powhattan...........	....	400 00	400 00
Robert Alexander........	St. Clairsville.....	220 00	988 00	1,208 00
Geo. W. Chalfant........	Kirkwood............	150 00	170 00	320 00
H. G. Blayney...........	Martinsville........	....	57 00	57 00
Wm. Gaston..............	Bellair.............	9,040 00	60 00	9,100 00
S. H. Wallace...........	Concord.............	....	325 00	325 00
D. H. Laverty...........	Weegee..............	....	5 00	5 00
R. Armstrong............	New Athens..........	165 00	25 00	190 00
John P. Caldwell........	Crab Apple..........	15 00	....	15 00
Wm. M. Ferguson.........	Washington..........	....	55 00	55 00
		$17,835 00	$2,547 13	$20,382 13

Churches not reported, 24.

PRESBYTERY OF CLEVELAND.

Ministers.	Churches.	Home Objects.	General Objects.	Total.
H. L. Hitchcock, D.D.....	West'rn Reserve College	....	$4,585 00	$4,585 00
W. H. Goodrich, D.D......	Cleveland, First.......	$20,000 00	26,652 00	46,652 00
E. Curtis..................	Newburgh............	1,100 00	150 00	1,250 00
James Eells, D.D..........	" Second.....	15,403 00	30,368 00	45,761 00
O. A. Lyman, D.D.........	" Euclid St...	15,323 00	15,100 00	30,423 00
E. B. Raffensberger........	" Westminster	1,300 00	5,800 00	7,100 00
J. N. McGiffert............	Ashtabula............	1,250 00	200 00	1,450 00
....	Burton................	....	510 00	510 00
Franklin Maginnis.........	Rome.................	372 00	82 00	454 00
D. K. Steele	Willoughby...........	2,000 00	....	2,000 00
Varnum Noyes............	Guilford..............	....	35 00	35 00
A. W. Knowlton...........	Strongsville..........	300 00	22 00	322 00
William B. Marsh.........	Bedford...............	....	500 00	500 00
" "	Northfield	400 00	185 00	585 00
....	Chester...............	....	150 00	150 00
....	Elyria................	....	366 00	366 00
Hubbard Lawrence........	Independence.........	37 00	....	37 00
H. V. Hitchcock.........	Streetsboro...........	....	55 00	55 00
Madison Elliot............	Grafton..............	237 00	30 00	267 00
Wm. F. Milliken..........	Orwell................	....	25 00	25 00
Anson Smyth............	North Presbyterian Church, Cleveland	400 00	100 00	500 00
R. H. Leonard............	Collamer, First Ch....	....	647 15	647 15
J. A. Skinner.............	MemorialCh.,Cleveland	1,800 00	300 00	2,100 00
		$59,922 00	$85,462 15	$145,884 15

Churches not reported, 13.

SYNOD OF COLORADO.

PRESBYTERY OF COLORADO.

Ministers.	Churches.	Home Objects.	General Objects.	Total.
Edward P. Wells..........	Denver, First	$814 99	....	$814 99
Wm. Y. Brown...........	" Stuart Memorial	3,600 00	....	3,600 00
J. Gibson Lowrie.........	Golden City...........	600 00	....	600 00
Geo. S. Adams...........	Pueblo	320 00	5 00	325 00
W. E. Hamilton..........	Black Hawk..........	....	20 00	20 00
Henry B. Gage	Colorado City.........	....	5 00	5 00
Charles M. Campbell......	Boulder Valley........	....	33 00	33 00
		$5,334 99	$63 00	$5,397 99

PRESBYTERY OF SANTA FE.

Ministers.	Churches.	Home Objects.	General Objects.	Total.
David F. McFarland.......	Santa Fe....	....	$30 00	$30 00
John A. Annin............	Las Vegas...........	....	25 00	25 00
			$55 00	$55 00

—o—

PRESBYTERY OF WYOMING.

Ministers.	Churches.	Home Objects.	General Objects.	Total.
F. L. Arnold..............	Laramie, Wy. Ter.....	$1.850 00	....	$1,850 00
W. G. Kephart	Cheyenne, " "	1,367 00	....	1,367 00
Edward E. Bayliss........	Corrinne, Utah.......	1,543 00	....	1,543 00
....	St. Vrain............	16 67	....	16 67
		$4,776 67	....	$4,776 67

SYNOD OF COLUMBUS.

PRESBYTERY OF ATHENS.

Ministers.	Churches.	Home Objects.	General Objects.	Total.
Julius Straus............	Watertown...........	....	$10 00	$10 00
Julius Straus............	Barlow	....	30 00	30 00
James Stickel............	Nelsonville......... ...	$237 00	5 00	242 00
H. B. Scott..............	Middleport...........	1,116 00	112 63	1,228 63
Chl. B. Taylor...........	Bashan	171 75	....	171 75
William Addy............	Marietta, Fourth St...	1,245 00	1,330 00	2,575 00
J. Noble S.S..........	Warren...............	....	115 00	115 00
E. W. Schroepl...........	Athens	2,465 00	25 00	2,490 00
Samuel Forbes...........	Beach Grove..........	....	5 00	5 00
		$5,234 75	$1,632 63	$6,867 38

Churches not reported, 17.

PRESBYTERY OF COLUMBUS.

Ministers.	Churches.	Home Objects.	General Objects.	Total.
David Kingery	Lower Liberty	$3,225 00		$3,225 00
	Columbus, First	1,732 00	$10 00	1,742 00
	Columbus, Second		1,922 54	1,922 54
A. J. Reynolds	Lithopolis	740 00		740 00
	Medway	175 00		175 00
	Greenfield	2,460 00		2,460 00
	Grove City		160 00	160 00
H. R. Hoisington	Circleville, First	1,099 00		1,099 00
	Lancaster	1,164 00		1,164 00
J. H. Stevens	Dublin		46 50	46 50
	Mount Stirling		300 00	300 00
J. H. Stevenson	Groveport	2,500 00		2,500 00
Levi P. Sabin	Central College	3,357 00		3,357 00
		$16,452 00	$2,439 04	$18,891 04

Churches not reported, 15.

——o——

PRESBYTERY OF MARION.

Ministers.	Churches.	Home Objects.	General Objects.	Total.
John W. Thompson	Berlin		$32 00	$32 00
Milton M. McMillin	Mount Gilead	$249 00	710 00	959 00
S. D. Smith	Richland	80 00		80 00
Henry Shedd	Little Mill Creek	200 00		200 00
S. D. Smith	Pisgah	20 00		20 00
R. F. Maclaren	Delaware		1,160 00	1,160 00
John McCutchan	Ashley		35 00	35 00
W. G. March	Marysville	2,459 68	282 50	2,742 18
J. L. Lower	Brown	81 00	19 00	100 00
E. W. Brown	Chesterville	900 00		900 00
C. H. Peeking	Radnor	1,400 00		1,400 00
S. D. Smith	Delhi	150 00		150 00
W. G. March	Milford Centre	4,473 68		4,473 68
Robert Wylie	Trenton	186 00		186 00
	Bloomfield	472 00	55 00	527 00
Henry Shedd	York	525 00	20 00	545 00
		$11,196 36	$2,313 50	$13,509 86

Churches not reported, 11.

PRESBYTERY OF WOOSTER.

Ministers.	Churches.	Home Objects.	General Objects.	Total.
Thomas Beer	Jeromeville	....	$215 00	$215 00
J. C. Gillam	Homesville	$200 00	166 00	366 00
Thomas K. Davis	Haysville	....	4,126 09	4,126 09
John O. Proctor	Lexington	240 00	137 00	377 00
John S. Atkinson	Wayne	....	21 00	21 00
D. Hall	Mansfield	2,800 00	5,000 00	7,800 00
T. P. Speer	West Salem	388 00	....	388 00
V. G. Sheeley	Dalton	390 00	580 00	970 00
E. B. Caldwell	East Hopewell	150 00	175 00	325 00
....	Blooming Grove	450 00	....	450 00
T. H. Barr	Jackson	400 00	10 00	410 00
J. C. Gillam	Shreve	....	51 00	51 00
Thomas K. Davis	McKay	....	74 00	74 00
John O. Proctor	Belleville	683 00	50 00	733 00
John S. Atkinson	Chester	....	22 00	22 00
....	Orrville	6,220 00	25 00	6,245 00
Franklin Eddy	Perrysville	120 00	179 00	299 00
S. W. Miller	Wooster	....	1,140 00	1,140 00
E. B. Caldwell	Nashville	200 00	50 00	250 00
John Robinson	Ashland	....	681 62	681 62
W. W. Anderson	Shelby	1,000 00	....	1,000 00
W. Jeffrey Park	Fredericksburg	1,800 00	345 00	2,145 00
A. S. Milholland	Millersburg	....	130 00	130 00
T. P. Speer	Congress	140 00	80 00	220 00
A. E. Thomson	Apple Creek	2,283 00	77 50	2,360 50
W. W. Anderson	Ontario	136 00	50 00	186 00
		$17,600 00	$13,390 21	$30,990 21

Churches not reported, 8.

——o——

PRESBYTERY OF ZANESVILLE.

Ministers.	Churches.	Home Objects.	General Objects.	Total.
W. E. Hunt	Coshocton	$2,600 00	$5 00	$2,605 00
H. M. Hervey	Newark, First	200 00	....	200 00
Howard Kingsbury	Newark, Second	900 00	20 00	920 00
A. S. Dudley	Granville	1,100 00	9,255 00	10,355 00
....	Zanesville, First	....	5 23	5 23
....	Zanesville, Second	....	50 00	50 00
H. C. MacBride	Ruraldale	....	5 23	5 23
James D. Walkinshaw	Mount Pleasant	....	7 00	7 00
R. W. Marquis	Keene	206 00	....	206 00
Andrew Thomas	Jersey	....	199 00	199 00
F. H. W. Benechert	Salem, Ger., Newark	....	95 00	95 00
W. B. Scarborough	Madison (Adams' Mills)	....	950 00	950 00
Timothy W. Howe	Pataskala	5,808 00	....	5,808 00
F. Broun	Muskingam	16 00	97 00	113 00
A. Kingsbury, D.D.	Putnam	....	13,765 50	13,765 50
....	Johnstown	....	110 00	110 00
J. Price Safford, D.D.	Brownsville	....	210 00	210 00
R. W. Marquis	Clarke	....	15 00	15 00
R. Hahn	Kirkersville, First	473 00	225 00	698 00
....	Batavia	100 00	50 00	150 00
		$11,403 00	$250,63 96	$36,466 96

Churches not reported, 37.

SYNOD OF ERIE.

PRESBYTERY OF ALLEGHENY.

Ministers.	Churches.	Home Objects.	General Objects.	Total.
John M. Smith	Highland	$431 00	....	$431 00
J. B. Bittenger, D.D.	Sewickley	9,500 00	$1,020 00	10,520 00
John Brown	Concord	500 00	....	500 00
James M. Shields	Bridgewater	....	316 70	316 70
E. E. Swift, D.D.	Allegheny, First	....	687 50	687 50
A. A. Hodge, D.D	Allegheny, North	8,570 00	65 00	8,635 00
John E. F. Launitz	Allegheny, First Ger.	260 18	27 00	287 18
J. V. Cellars	Providence (Allegheny)	375 00	25 00	400 00
D. P. Lowary	Beaver	....	383 25	383 25
R. S. Van Cleve	Leitsdale	5,000 00	356 00	5,356 00
G. M. Potter	Pine Creek, First	164 00	....	164 00
....	Millvale	1,000 00	....	1,000 00
Levi Risher	Plains	900 00	....	900 00
W. C. Falconer	Sharpsburg	4,200 00	50 00	4,250 00
W. P. Moore	Manchester, Allegheny, Second	1,770 00	180 00	1,950 00
M. L. Wortman	Emsworth	200 00	....	200 00
" "	Industry	3,000 00	....	3,000 00
John Kerr	Allegheny (Valley)	1,900 00	100 00	2,000 00
....	Greenfield	....	10 00	10 00
....	Clarksville	1,737 00	....	1,737 00
....	Belleview	300 00	....	300 00
		$39,807 18	$3,220 45	$43,027 63

Churches not reported, 15.

—o—

PRESBYTERY OF BUTLER.

Ministers.	Churches.	Home Objects.	General Objects.	Total.
R. B. Walker, D.D.	Plain Grove	$519 33	$55 68	$575 01
J. R. Coulter	Scrub Grass	....	172 00	172 00
J. McPherrin	Westminster	....	73 50	73 50
J. H. Marshall	North Butler	....	32 00	32 00
T. B. Van Eman	Clintonville	....	89 59	89 59
S. L. Johnson	Portersville	366 50	....	366 50
....	New Salem	....	91 25	91 25
....	Centre	....	47 00	47 00
J. McPherrin	Buffalo	....	106 00	106 00
W. D. Patton	Harrisville	5,000 00	....	5,000 00
S. L. Johnson	Zelienople	....	9 00	9 00
Robt. McMillan	Rich Hill	1,100 00	....	1,100 00
W. T. Dickson	Pine Grove	193 00	67 00	260 00
S. Williams	Muddy Creek	....	79 00	79 00
J. H. Marshall	Concord	109 00	141 00	250 00
W. D. Patton	Amity	305 00	125 00	430 00
D. C. Cooper	Centreville	1,340 00	....	1,340 00
E. Ogden	Middlesex	60 25	67 00	127 25
J. Coulter	Martinsburgh	125 00	....	125 00
....	Bull Creek	....	8 00	8 00
....	Sunbury	....	45 15	45 15
		$9,118 08	$1,208 17	$10,326 25

Churches not reported, 8.

PRESBYTERY OF CLARION.

Ministers.	Churches.	Home Objects.	General Objects.	Total.
....	Beech Woods..........	....	$49 75	$49 75
J. S. Elder...............	Clarion...............	$1,746 00	10 00	1,756 00
T. J. Milford............	Concord..............	100 00	50 00	150 00
J. Caldwell..............	Perry................	....	30 00	30 00
Joseph Mateer...........	Licking..............	257 00	174 00	431 00
J. S. Elder...............	New Rehoboth........	279 00	17 00	296 00
John McMillan...........	Mount Pleasant.......	20,000 00	5,000 00	25,000 00
Andrew Virtue...........	Academia............	....	50 00	50 00
Andrew Virtue...........	Emlenton............	200 00	....	200 00
J. Milton Hamilton.......	Pisgah...............	2,200 00	....	2,200 00
J. J. Marks, D.D.........	Brookville...........	2,200 00	....	2,200 00
Joseph Mateer...........	Leatherwood..........	580 00	25 00	605 00
Andrew Virtue...........	Rockland............	150 00	....	150 00
T. J. Milford............	Callensburg..........	478 40	20 00	498 40
....	Oak Grove...........	79 50	10 00	89 50
....	Maysville............	1,500 00	....	1,500 00
....	Reynoldsville.........	2,000 00	....	2,000 00
T. J. Milford..........	Parker's Station (new church)............	1,345 05	....	1,345 05
		$33,114 95	$5,435 75	$38,550 70

Churches not reported, 12.

——o——

PRESBYTERY OF KITTANNING.

Ministers.	Churches.	Home Objects.	General Objects.	Total.
W. W. Woodend	Saltsburgh............	$3,379 95	$352 20	$3,732 15
John Caruther............	Marion................	4,700 00	....	4,700 00
....	Centre................	88 00	....	88 00
....	Apollo...............	1,037 00	....	1,037 00
Franklin Orr.............	Bethel	40 00	85 00	125 00
C. Moore.................	Mount Pleasant........	1,750 00	....	1,750 00
Franklin Orr.............	Jacksonville..........	100 00	170 00	270 00
G. W. Mechlin............	Glade Run............	641 00	411 00	1,052 00
D. J. Irwin..............	Ebenezer.............	8,500 00	96 00	8,596 00
T. D. Ewing..............	Kittanning...........	....	5,327 25	5,327 00
A. McElwain.............	Indiana..............	....	1,747 00	1,747 00
Wm. F. Morgan...........	Rural Valley..........	5 00	....	5 00
S. H. Holliday...........	Brady's Bend..........	480 00	25 00	505 00
H. Magill................	Mahoning.............	732 00	20 00	752 00
C. Moore.................	Smicksburgh..........	....	25 00	25 00
....	Pine Run.............	713 00	....	713 00
A. S. Thompson..........	Worthington	2,250 00	....	2,250 00
J. J. Francis.............	Freeport.............	3,000 00	....	3,000 00
Wm. M. Kain............	Slate Lick............	1,017 00	....	1,017 00
D. G. Robinson...........	Homer................	1,500 00	....	1,500 00
S. A. Hughes.............	Lawrenceburg.........	2,000 00	23 00	2,023 00
H. Magill................	Concord	52 00	....	55 00
		$31,984 95	$8,281 45	$40,266 40

Churches not reported, 23.

PRESBYTERY OF ERIE.

Ministers.	Churches.	Home Objects.	General Objects.	Total.
A. H. Carrier	Erie, First	$4,128 00		$4,128 00
Jas. Otis Denniston	Erie, Park	3,200 00		3,200 00
John McMaster	Pittsfield	1,000 00	$160 00	1,160 00
John McMaster	Garland	1,700 00		1,700 00
Robt. H. Reeves	Sunville	1,200 00		1,200 00
William Elliott	Cherrytree	200 00		200 00
N. McFetridge	Oil City	8,950 00	1,600 00	10,550 00
J. E. Wright	Greenville	4,500 00		4,500 00
R. Craighead	Meadville, Second	2,410 00	25 00	2,435 00
S. J. M. Eaton, D.D.	Franklin	750 00	339 00	1,089 00
O. A. Elliott	Fairfield	300 00		300 00
J. R. Findley	Mercer, First	8,756 00		8,756 00
Wm. M. Robinson	Mercer, Second	1,000 00	26 00	1,026 00
F. V. Warren	Wattsburg	795 00		795 00
E. B. Chamberlain	Springfield	1,000 00		1,000 00
Wm. H. Adams	East Green	208 00		208 00
J. H. Edwards	Tidioute	3,700 00	270 00	3,970 00
M. M. Shirley	Waterloo	183 00		183 00
R. L. Stewart	Harmonsburgh		169 25	169 25
G. W. Cleaveland	Harbor Creek	5,349 00		5,349 00
John W. McCune	Coolspring	600 00	33 00	633 00
William Elliott	Kerr's Hill	50 00		50 00
O. A. Elliott	Cochranton	105 00	10 00	115 00
W. A. Rankin	Warren, First	5,200 00		5,200 00
R. L. Stewart	Conneautville	1,161 98		1,161 98
J. M. Gillette	Union	3,100 00		3,100 00
John T. Axtoby	North East		500 00	500 00
M. M. Shirley	Mount Pleasant	127 00		127 00
A. C. Junkin	Fairview	2,004 00	20 00	2,024 00
David Patton	Petroleum Centre	100 00	1,076 52	1,176 52
	Milledgeville	275 00	90 00	365 00
W. L. Wright	Westminster	1,800 00		1,800 00
William Elliott	Dempseytown	100 00		100 00
	Sugar Grove	360 00		360 00
J. W. McCune	Salem		43 00	43 00
H. Magill	Concord	6 00	168 00	174 00
Wm. McMichael	Greenfield		10 00	10 00
Robt. M. Brown	Rouseville	1,300 00		1,300 00
Wm. Grassie	Edinboro'		450 00	450 00
Wm. McMichael	Evansburgh	1,000 00		1,000 00
C. C. Kimball	Central Church of Erie.	13,382 00		13,382 00
	Waterford		28 00	28 00
	Pleasantville	6,000 00		6,000 00
		$85,999 98	$5,017 77	$91,017 75

Churches not reported, 17.

—o—

PRESBYTERY OF SHENANGO.

Ministers.	Churches.	Home Objects.	General Objects.	Total.
D. X. Jenkin, D.D.	New Castle, First	$1,540 00	$921 00	$2,461 00
R. J. Graves	Sharon	158 25		158 25
Robt. McMillan	Hermon	2,500 00		2,500 00
	West Middlesex		30 19	30 19
D. C. Reed	Unity	815 00	223 00	1,038 00
Wm. M. Taylor	Westfield	270 00	884 00	1,154 00
John K. Andrew	Mahoning	1,504 00		1,504 00
H. N. Potter	Mount Pleasant	130 00		130 00
J. B. Miller	Little Beaver		275 00	275 00
J. M. Mealy	Neshannock	200 00	550 00	750 00
		$7,117 25	$2,883 19	$10,000 44

Churches not reported, 10.

SYNOD OF GENEVA.

PRESBYTERY OF CAYUGA.

Ministers.	Churches.	Home Objects.	General Objects.	Total.
Charles Hawley, D.D......	Auburn, First.........	$16,000 00	$1,000 00	$17,000 00
S. W. Boardman, D.D.....	" Second.......	2,040 00	1,960 00	4,000 00
Henry Fowler.	" Central.......	6,700 00	....	6,700 00
*W. W. Howard, D.D.....	Aurora................	28,000 00	20,235 00	48,235 00
J. S. Jewell..............	Genoa, First..........	5,200 00	....	5,200 00
G. G. Smith..............	" Second........	1,000 00	25 00	1,025 00
A. R. Hewitt..............	Weedsport.............	6,040 00	....	6,040 00
Albert F. Lyle............	Springport............	300 00	....	300 00
C. A. Conant..............	Genoa, Third..........	1,400 00	....	1,400 00
G. P. Sewall..............	Cayuga................	820 60	227 30	1,047 90
Wallace B. Lucas.........	Meridian..............	1,063 00	1,016 00	2,079 00
Chas. Anderson...........	Sennett...............	700 00	....	700 00
J. V. C. Nellis............	Dryden................	760 00	126 00	886 00
		$70,020 60	$24,553 30	$94,575 90

*Deceased.

Churches not reported, 7.

——o——

PRESBYTERY OF CHEMUNG.

Ministers.	Churches.	Home Objects.	General Objects.	Total.
Robert E. Willson.........	Havana...............	$5,240 00	....	$5,240 00
W. E. Knox, D.D.........	Elmira, First..........	200 00	$6,096 00	6,296 00
Wm. Atwood..............	Big Flatts.............	275 00	171 00	446 00
J. B. Beaumont...........	Waverley..............	4,100 00	25 00	4,125 00
Walter S. Drysdale........	Dundee................	400 00	....	400 00
A. O. Peloubet............	Mecklinburgh.........	440 00	....	440 00
Calvin Case...............	Hector................	175 00	....	175 00
Charles Chapman.........	Mead's Creek..........	570 00	....	570 00
E. W. Twichell............	Burdett...............	....	82 00	82 00
Nathan M. Sherwood......	Elmira, Second........	2,500 00	1,300 00	3,800 00
		$13,903 00	$7,705 00	$21,608 00

Churches not reported, 8.

PRESBYTERY OF GENEVA.

Ministers.	Churches.	Home Objects.	General Objects.	Total.
S. H. Gridley, D.D.	Waterloo	$1,550 00	$200 00	$1,750 00
E. H. Stratton	Canoga	510 00	.....	510 00
A. A. Wood, D.D.	Geneva	180 00	1,218 00	1,398 00
A. T. Young	Oak's Corners	1,000 00	.....	1,000 00
A. H. Parmelee	Seneca Castle	.....	5 00	5 00
B. M. Goldsmith	Benton	383 50	60 00	443 50
D. D. McCall	Phelps	1,000 00	160 00	1,160 00
George Patton	Seneca	1,900 00	.....	1,900 00
C. T. White, D.D.	Branchport	327 00	.....	327 00
Theodore F. White	Ithaca	39 00	2,154 00	2,193 00
J. D. Krum	Seneca Falls	20,000 00	100 00	20,100 00
N. S. Lourie	Gorham	2,429 00	.....	2,429 00
David Magie, D.D.	Penn Yan	.....	.....	.....
H. W. Torrance	Ovid	.....	.....	.....
.....	Victor	6,500 00	.....	6,500 00
S. H. Thompson, Ph.D.	Canandaigua	20,000 00	.....	20,000 00
.....	Honeoye	.....	500 00	500 00
.....	Hopewell	.....	10 00	10 00
		$55,718 50	$4,316 00	$60,034 50

Churches not reported, 10.

—o—

PRESBYTERY OF STEUBEN.

Ministers.	Churches.	Home Objects.	General Objects.	Total.
J. M. Platt	Bath	$3,400 00	$230 00	$3,630 00
Joel Wakeman, D.D.	Campbell	1,750 00	.....	1,750 00
W. A. Niles, D.D.	Corning	16,481 00	50 00	16,531 00
Z. N. Bradbury	Pultney	1,800 00	.....	1,800 00
D. Henry Palmer	Prattsburgh	700 00	50 00	750 00
P. H. Burghardt	Painted Post	6,300 00	.....	6,300 00
James H. Board	Howard	1,400 00	.....	1,400 00
Alex. Gulick	Jasper	3,500 00	.....	3,500 00
Darwin Chichester	Hammondsport	475 00	.....	475 00
.....	Woodhull	25 00	.....	25 00
.....	Cohocton	1,600 00	.....	1,600 00
.....	Wheeler	2,055 00	.....	2,055 00
Milton Waldo, D.D.	Hornellsville	5,000 00	50 00	5,050 00
.....	Arkport	476 56	.....	476 56
Lewis F. Laine	Canisteo	.....	96 00	96 00
		$44,962 56	$476 00	$45,388 56

Churches not reported, 13.

PRESBYTERY OF LYONS.

Ministers.	Churches.	Home Objects.	General Objects.	Total.
Horace Eaton, D.D.	Palmyra	....	$1,411 50	$1,411 50
Samuel S. Pomeroy	Savannah	$1,365 00	....	1,365 00
James Ireland	Sodus	600 00	....	600 00
E. W Kellogg	Wolcott, Second	1,600 00	....	1,600 00
....	East Palmyra	1,500 00	....	1,500 00
W. L. Page	Wolcott, First	4,000 00	....	4,000 00
J. R. Young	Clyde (Galen)	19,500 00	....	19,500 00
W. Young	Rose	150 00	50 00	200 00
N. Bosworth	Williamson	650 00	....	650 00
Henry L. Doolittle	Huron	703 00	....	703 00
A. C. Sewall	Newark	1,195 00	5 00	1,200 00
		$31,263 00	$1,466 50	$32,729 50

SYNOD OF HARRISBURG.

PRESBYTERY OF CARLISLE.

Ministers.	Churches.	Home Objects.	General Objects.	Total.
Thos. Creigh, D.D	Mercersburg	$300 00	$800 00	$1,100 00
A. K. Nelson	St. Thomas	235 00	....	225 00
C. P. Wing, D.D	Carlisle, First	5,785 35	214 65	6,000 00
George Norcross	Carlisle, Second	20,000 00	....	20,000 00
J. F. Kennedy	Fayetteville	50 25	35 00	85 25
D. C. Meeker	Dauphin	1,095 00	....	1,095 00
A. D. Mitchell	Paxton	....	137 25	137 25
I. N. Hays	Chambersburg, Central	4,013 00	....	4.013 00
J. A. Crawford	Chambersburg, F'g S'g	....	6,000 00	6,000 00
W. A. West	Upper Path Valley	2,340 00	100 00	2,440 00
J. Smith Gordon	Lower Path Valley	130 95	223 10	254 05
J. Smith Gordon	Burnt Cabins	58 00	26 50	84 50
T. H. Robinson, D.D	Harrisburg, Market Sq.	8,400 00	2,380 00	10,780 00
A. K. Strong, D.D	Harrisburg, Pine St.	10,012 28	1,643 00	11,655 28
Chas. A. Wyeth	Harrisburg, Seventh St.	....	52 00	52 00
....	Greencastle	200 00	4,233 50	4,433 50
Henry L. Rex	Middletown	225 00	....	225 00
James S. Woodburn	Dickinson	310 00	....	310 00
William Thomson	Duncannon	2,425 00	....	2,425 00
William Thomson	Shermansdale	....	14 50	14 50
D. K. Richardson	Middle Spring	2,150 00	110 00	2,260 00
W. S. Van Cleve	Great Conewago	....	158 00	158 00
W. S. Van Cleve	Lower Marsh Creek	358 00	....	358 00
S. W. Pomeroy	McConnelsburg	639 00	....	639 00
S. W. Pomeroy	Green Hill	300 00	500 00	800 00
S. W. Pomeroy	Wells' Valley	161 00	....	161 00
W. H. Hillis	Gettysburg	307 50	387 50	695 00
S. W. Reigart	Mechanicsburg	375 00	425 00	800 00
Ebenezer Erskine, D.D.	Big Spring	3,000 00	....	3,000 00
John Edgar	Bloomfield	4,800 00	....	4,800 00
W. N. Geddes	Waynesboro	....	140 00	140 00
A. S. Thorne	Robert Kennedy Ch.	800 00	100 00	900 00
		$68,470 33	$17,680 00	$86,150

Churches not reported, 12.

PRESBYTERY OF NORTHUMBERLAND.

Ministers.	Churches.	Home Objects.	General Objects.	Total.
I. Grier, D.D.	Buffalo		$45 00	$45 00
S. C. McElroy	Derry	$1,300 00		1,300 00
Wm. Simonton	Williamsport, First		400 00	400 00
	Williamsport, Second	6,000 00	25 00	6,025 00
A. D. Hawn	Williamsport, Third	750 00		750 00
D. J. Waller	Bloomsburg	3,000 00		3,000 00
W. G. E. Agnew	Bald Eagle and Nittany	860 00		860 00
Joseph Stevens	Jersey Shore		3,008 71	3,008 71
Joseph Nesbitt	Great Island	18,600 00		18,600 00
A. B. Jack	Mahoning	3,000 00		3,000 00
Sam'l P. Herron	Warrior Run	600 00		600 00
L. J. Milliken	Sunbury	20,500 00		20,500 00
H. G. Finney	Lycoming Centre	300 00	150 00	450 00
Nathaniel Spear	Rhorsburg	377 02		377 02
B. T. Jones	Lewisburg	2,700 00		2,700 00
R. H. Van Pelt	Grove	12,500 00		12,500 00
S. C. McElroy	Washingtonville	825 00		825 00
L. L. Haughawout	Washington	1,875 82		1,875 82
John Thomas	New Columbia	4,000 00		4,000 00
	Muncy	150 00	185 00	335 00
J. D. Reardon	Mifflinburg	1,500 00		1,500 00
J. D. Reardon	New Berlin	100 00		100 00
J. D. Reardon	Hartleton	100 00	5 00	105 00
F. F. Kolb	McEwensville	542 00		542 00
J. Dickson	Berwick	1,000 00		1,000 00
J. C. Caldwell	Lycoming	600 00	350 00	950 00
Alvin C. Campbell	North Point & Renovo	1,500 00		1,500 00
S. M. Gould	Emporium	260 00		260 00
P. B. Marr	Pennsdale	2,600 00		2,600 00
Thos. S. Dewing	Shamokintown	830 00	720 00	1,550 00
W. G. E. Agnew	Beech Creek	3,200 00		3,200 00
		$89,569 84	$4,888 71	$94,458 55

Churches not reported, 15.

——o——

PRESBYTERY OF WELLSBORO.

Ministers.	Churches.	Home Objects.	General Objects.	Total.
J. F. Calkins	Wellsboro	$1,500 00		$1,500 00
Henry Neill, Jr.	Lawrenceville	2,500 00		2,500 00
Samuel A. Rawson	Beecher's Island	67 00		67 00
G. R. H. Shumway	Fall Brook		$10 00	10 00
P. L. Landis	Coudersport	300 00	30 00	330 00
George Morton	Arnot		10 00	10 00
Joseph A. Rosseel	Covington	2,100 00		2,100 00
John Cairnes	Elkland	2,500 00		2,500 00
Joseph A. Rosseel	Mansfield	2,500 00		2,500 00
		$11,467 00	$50 00	$11,517 00

Churches not reported, 6.

PRESBYTERY OF HUNTINGDON.

Ministers.	Churches.	Home Objects.	General Objects.	Total.
Matthew Allison	Mifflinstown & Lost Cr.	$493 55	$396 90	$890 45
....	Mapletown	....	....	....
W. J. Gibson, D.D	East Freedom	136 00	....	136 00
W. J. Gibson, D.D	Martinsburg	....	60 00	60 00
N. G. White	Williamsburg	1,100 00	....	1,100 00
John H. Sargent	Bradford	....	5 00	5 00
....	Kylertown	....	20 00	20 00
Wm. Prideaux	Beulah	1,714 00	....	1,714 00
Robert Hamill, D.D	Sinking Creek	150 00	15 00	165 00
Robert Hamill, D.D	Spring Creek	7,500 00	....	7,500 00
G. W. Zahniser	Huntingdon	18,355 00	80 00	18,435 00
R. M. Wallace	Altoona, First	356 75	200 00	556 75
W. J. Chichester	Altoona, Second	23,000 00	....	23,000 00
W. T. Wylie	Bellefonte	12,025 00	6,362 50	18,387 50
J. W. White	Milroy	115 00	....	115 00
J. H. Mathers	Logan's Valley	....	70 00	70 00
R. F. Wilson	Bedford	1,200 00	....	1,200 00
D. H. Barron	Hollidaysburg	5,756 13	....	5,756 13
....	Alexandria	442 00	40 00	482 00
....	Yellow Creek	....	1,000 00	1,000 00
....	Osceola	883 79	....	883 79
Wm. M. Burchfield	Curwinsville	150 00	....	150 00
W. O. Wright	Milesburg	120 00	....	120 00
Jno. C. Wilhelm	Schellsburg	180 00	10 00	190 00
J. E. Kearns	Upper Tuscarora	135 75	20 00	155 75
J. E. Kearns	Peru	777 00	....	777 00
H. S. Butler	Clearfield	5,044 00	330 55	5,374 55
R. M. Campbell	West Kishacoquillas	320 00	....	320 00
J. J. Coale	Sinking Valley	20 85	....	20 85
J. C. Wilhelm	Shaver's Creek	15 00	....	15 00
J. H. Sargent	Phillipsburg	....	11 00	11 00
S. S. Wallon	Middle Tuscarora	700 00	....	700 00
S. M. Moore	Tyrone	876 00	45 03	921 03
....	Lick Run	....	10 00	10 00
....	Spring Mills	225 00	....	225 00
J. C. Kelly	Spruce Creek	....	223 67	223 67
....	Buffalo Run	1,100 00	20 00	1,120 00
		$82,890 82	$8,919 65	$91,810 47

Churches not reported, 23.

SYNOD OF ILLINOIS CENTRAL.

PRESBYTERY OF BLOOMINGTON.

Ministers.	Churches.	Home Objects.	General Objects.	Total.
John McClean	Bloomington, First	$1.620 00	....	$1,620 00
J. W. Dinsmore	Bloomington, Second	2,600 00	....	2,600 00
C. J. Pitkin	Cerro Gordo	80 00	....	80 00
John S. Frame	Champaign	6,603 00	....	6.603 00
M. M. Travis	Chenoa	1,899 21	....	1,899 21
....	Chatsworth	394 00	....	394 00
J. A. Piper	Clinton	....	450 00	450 00
A. L. Brooks	Danville	4,080 00	570 00	4,650 00
S. Wilson, D.D.	El Paso	127 00	....	127 00
J. O. Hough	Farmer City	30 00	....	30 00
....	Gilman	....	100 00	100 00
W. R. Glen	Heyworth	....	124 00	124 00
David R. Love	Lexington	2,700 00	3 00	2,703 00
S. H. Stevenson	Middleport	....	27 00	27 00
D. W. Evans	Minonk	3,300 00	....	3,300 00
J. Rogers Wilson	Normall	800 00	12 00	812 00
M. B. Lowrie	Onarga	800 00	15 00	815 00
J. S. MacConnell	Pontiac	36 00	225 00	261 00
W. B. Keeling	Reading	1,200 00	....	1,200 00
R. Conover	Towanda	....	206 50	206 50
W. C. Smith	Urbana	3,500 00	....	3.500 00
S. V. McKee	Waynesville	400 00	....	400 00
Horace McVey	Winona	107 54	19 46	127 00
W. N. Steele	Rossville	3,400 00	....	3,400 00
		$33,676 75	$1,751 96	$35,428 71

Churches not reported, 20.

—o—

PRESBYTERY OF PEORIA.

Ministers.	Churches.	Home Objects.	General Objects.	Total.
....	Peoria, First	$9,725 00	....	$9,725 00
H. V. D. Nevins	Peoria, Second	1,000 00	$30 00	1,030 00
John Weston	Peoria, Calvary Mission	5,000 00	....	5.000 00
Horace C. Hovey	Peoria, Fulton St.	500 00	1,140 00	1,640 00
John Winn	Henry	....	130 00	130 00
....	Princeville	....	....	....
L. Pratt	Galesburg	....	925 00	925 00
J. R. Reasoner	Elmwood	....	17 50	17 50
William Keiry	Brunswick	200 00	....	200 00
William Keiry	Salem	532 00	....	532 00
Edward H. Curtis	Lacon	300 00	....	300 00
D. G. Bradford	Knoxville	932 84	129 15	1,061 99
Charles Phillip	Low Point	....	75 00	75 00
....	Brimfield	3,318 00	....	3,318 00
....	Oneida	290 00	....	290 00
J. F. Magill	Lewistown	....	410 00	410 00
....	John Knox	175 00	....	175 00
R. C. Colmery	Delavan	1,003 45	....	1,003 45
Isaac A. Cornelison	Washington	4,000 00	16 00	4,016 00
		$26,976 29	$2,872 65	$29,848 94

Churches not reported, 18.

PRESBYTERY OF SCHUYLER.

Ministers.	Churches.	Home Objects.	General Objects.	Total.
R. C. Mathews, D.D.	Monmouth	$527 00		$527 00
J. H. Marshall	Young America	700 00		700 00
Andrus F. Ashley	Good Hope	450 00		450 00
W. C. Burchard	Rushville		$427 00	427 00
T. Campbell	Camp Point	585 46		585 46
Alex. Duncan	Mt. Sterling, First	420 00		420 00
W. W. Whipple	Clayton	1,110 00		1,110 00
J. A. Priest	Quincey	3,026 86	125 00	3,151 86
M. Waldenmeyer	Appanoose	600 00		600 00
	Pontoosuck	425 00		425 00
J. N. Crittenden	Warsaw	500 00		500 00
	Plymouth	56 70		56 70
A. S. Powell	Brooklyn	30 00		30 00
A. S. Powell	Huntsville	2,108 00		2,108 00
J. Leslie Irwin	Independence	1,700 00		1,700 00
Thos. M. Walker	Fountain Green	4,000 00		4,000 00
Henry C. Mullan	Ebenezer	590 00		590 00
H. K. McComb	Macomb	1,225 00		1,225 00
G. N. Johnson	Carthage			
	Doddsville	70 00	25 00	95 00
Preston W. Thomson	Camp Creek	181 00		181 00
W. H. Smith	Perry		1,500 00	1,500 00
R. T. McMahon	Bardolph	80 00	301 00	381 00
J. Leslie Irwin	Ellington	2,000 00		2,000 00
H. Hanson	Keithsburg	353 00		353 00
" "	Oquawka	63 00	10 00	73 00
		$20,801 02	$2,388 00	$23,189 02

Churches not reported, 26.

—o—

PRESBYTERY OF SPRINGFIELD.

Ministers.	Churches.	Home Objects.	General Objects.	Total.
Rev. J. A. Reed	Springfield, First	$15,000 00		$15,000 00
G. H. Robertson	Springfield, Second	6,660 00		6,660 00
H. M. Paynter	Springfield, Third	10,000 00		10,000 00
F. I. Moffatt	Irish Grove	117 00		117 00
John Crozier	North Sangamon	785 00		785 00
J. A. Hood	Maroa	1,600 00		1,600 00
S. J. Bogle	Mason City	6,000 00		6,000 00
M. P. Ormsby	Winchester	300 00	$80 00	380 00
John H. Harris	Chatham	820 00		820 00
W. D. Sanders, D.D	Pisgah	500 00	1,350 00	1,850 00
L. M. Glover, D.D	Jacksonville, First		10,000 00	10,000 00
W. W. Harsha, D.D	Jacksonville, Central	18,000 00		18,000 00
D. H. Hamilton, D.D	Jacksonville, Westmin'r	1,500 00		1,500 00
	Brush Creek	2,700 00		2,700 00
		$63,982 00	$11,430 00	$75,412 00

Churches not reported, 19.

SYNOD OF ILLINOIS NORTH.

PRESBYTERY OF FREEPORT.

Ministers.	Churches.	Home Objects.	General Objects.	Total.
John McLean	Galena, First	$1,415 00	$207 50	$1,622 50
A. C. Smith	Galena, South	1,100 00	573 74	1,673 74
John Leirer	Galena, German	197 00	......	197 00
D. R. Eddy	Belvidere	450 00	40 75	490 75
......	Lena	......	8 15	8 15
Mead Holmes	Lawrence	1,100 00	200 00	1,300 00
Wm. A. Gay	Winnebago	1,950 00	300 00	2,250 00
J. M. Linn	Rock Run	535 00	20 00	555 00
J. M. Linn	Cedarville	76 75	......	76 75
......	Zion	......	34 00	34 00
T. C. Easton	Willow Creek	10,000 00	......	10,000 00
R. L. Adams	Harvard	1,045 00	......	1,045 00
Isaac E. Carey	Freeport, First	10,000 00	......	10,000 00
Geo. Elliot	Freeport, Second	200 00	100 00	300 00
A. J. Leyenberger	Rockford, First	3,627 00	335 00	3,962 00
Wm. S. Curtis, D.D.	Rockford, Westminster	500 00	50 00	550 00
Joseph Braddock	Middle Creek	......	......	......
J. M. Stone	Hanover	......	......	......
Sam'l C. Hay	Woodstock	......	350 00	350 00
F. C. Eastman	Linn and Hebron	340 00	......	340 00
John H. Carpenter	Marengo	1,200 00	......	1,200 00
		$33,735 75	$2,219 14	$35,954 89

Churches not reported, 17.

—o—

PRESBYTERY OF OTTAWA.

Ministers.	Churches.	Home Objects.	General Objects.	Total.
Thomas Galt	Aurora	$869 00	......	$869 00
James McLeod	Morris	1,670 00	......	1,670 00
Albert F. Hale	Somonauk	10 00	......	10 00
John Ustick	Earlville	125 00	$13 00	138 00
H. A. Barclay	Oswego	......	52 00	52 00
S. E. Vance	Granville	251 50	......	251 50
S. H. Weller	Mendotta	1,230 00	......	1,230 00
......	Troy Grove	2,200 00	4 00	2,204 00
D. Fletcher	Elgin	5,600 00	20 00	5,620 00
S. E. Smith	Gardner	1,500 00	......	1,500 00
E. L. Hurd, D.D	Sandwich	1,275 00	500 00	1,775 00
L. Y. Hays	Ottawa	4,500 00	......	4,500 00
Arthur Rose	Union Grove	......	85 00	85 00
......	Clinton Centre	......	13 00	13 00
Alex. S. Peck	Wyoming	75 00	......	75 00
W. W. Wells	Waltham	766 00	347 00	1,113 00
S. E. Smith	Vienna	2,800 00	......	2,800 00
W. C. MacDougall	Plato, First Ch	580 00	......	580 00
......	Plato, Second Ch	199 18	......	199 18
		$23,650 68	$1,034 00	$24,684 68

Churches not reported, 5.

PRESBYTERY OF CHICAGO.

Ministers.	Churches.	Home Objects.	General Objects.	Total.
Arthur Mitchell...........	Chicago, First........	$8,600 00	$3,980 00	$12,580 00
R. W. Patterson, D.D.	Chicago, Second......	....	17,124 50	17,124 50
A. E. Kittredge..........	Chicago, Third........	15.000 00	300 00	15,300 00
John McLeish............	Chicago, Seventh.....	560 00	....	560 00
Lewis H. Reid............	Chicago, Eighth......	1,400 00	5 00	1.405 00
Rev. A. Eddy.............	Chicago, Ninth........	1,700 00	....	1,700 00
David Swing..............	Chicago, Fourth......	....	5.000 00	5,000 00
Daniel Lord..............	Chicago, Calvary......	30,000 00	200 00	30,200 00
....	Chicago, Olivet.......	13,500 00	2,500 00	16,000 00
Robt. Patterson, D.D......	Chicago, Jefferson Pk.	1,450 00	1,200 00	2,650 00
Wm. M. Blackburn, D.D...	Chicago, Fullerton Ave.	3,693 45	2,100 00	5,793 45
J. H. Walker.............	Chicago, Reunion......	250 00	....	250 00
John H. Brown, D.D......	Chicago, 31st St.......	2,255 90	2,500 00	4,755 90
David S. Johnson.........	Chicago, Hyde Park...	11,500 00	12,750 00	24,250 00
N. Barrett...............	Dunton...............	85 00	299 00	384 00
C. F. Waldecker..........	Wheeling.............	200 00	....	200 00
P. Boudreault............	St. Anne, Second......	301 50	....	301 50
J. H. Barnard............	Kankakee.............	1,949 00	....	1,949 00
P. L. Carden.............	Manteno..............	100 00	....	100 00
Jas. H. Taylor............	Lake Forest...........	....	11,517 05	11,517 05
Geo. H. Coit.............	Wilmington...........	....	30 00	30 00
H. D. Jenkins............	Joliet, Central........	2,000 00	300 00	2,300 00
J. C. Myers..............	Will..................	149 00	....	149 00
Geo. C. Noyes............	Evanston, First Ch....	2,000 00	....	2,000 00
James Bassett............	Englewood............	2,800 00	1,000 00	3,800 00
E. R. Davis..............	Thornton Station......	550 00	....	550 00
Thomas L. Sexton........	Peotone..............	935 00	....	935 00
E. Van Noorden..........	Noble St., Holland....	400 00	100 00	500 00
		$101,378 85	$60,905 55	$162,284 40

Churches not reported, 6.

——o——

PRESBYTERY OF ROCK RIVER.

Ministers.	Churches.	Home Objects.	General Objects.	Total.
John Griffen.............	Newton...............	....	$6 60	$6 60
J. C. Barr...............	Geneseo..............	....	10 00	10 00
Josiah Milligan...........	Princeton, First Ch....	$791 83	1,081 75	1,873 58
Josiah Leonard...........	Garden Plains........	486 96	....	486 96
Meade C. Williams........	Sterling..............	1,070 00	200 00	1,270 00
T. R. Johnson............	Edgington............	1,300 00	....	1,300 00
J. S. McClung............	Calvary..............	3,708 00	....	3,708 00
W. C. Magner............	Woodhull.............	200 00	....	200 00
Henry Keigwin...........	Fulton...............	550 00	110 00	660 00
T. G. Scott..............	Malden...............	560 00	....	560 00
John Griffen.............	Albany...............	350 00	....	350 00
....	Sharon...............	150 00	....	150 00
....	Coal Valley...........	150 00	....	150 00
W. F. Wood..............	Rochelle.............	213 00	....	213 00
E. C. Sickles............	Dixon................	3,500 00	....	3,500 00
B. Shields Sloan.........	Edwards..............	1,000 00	....	1,000 00
W. S. Dool..............	Millersburg...........	3,700 00	....	3,700 00
H. A. Newell............	Rock Island..........	....	163 00	163 00
R. L. Adams.............	Andover.............	300 00	321 75	621 75
F. A. Shearer............	Aledo, First Ch.......	4,000 00	....	4,000 00
Henry W. Fisk...........	Beulah...............	310 00	....	310 00
Wm. S. Dool.............	Peniel................	3,900 00	....	3,900 00
		$26,239 79	$1,893 10	$28,132 89

Churches not reported, 16.

SYNOD OF ILLINOIS SOUTH.

PRESBYTERY OF ALTON.

Ministers.	Churches.	Home Objects.	General Objects.	Total.
W. R. Adams	Plainview	$40 00	....	$40 00
Robert Stewart	Troy	4,100 00	....	4,100 00
George I. King, D.D	Jerseyville	946 50	$147 00	1,093 50
L. I. Root	Upper Alton	235 00	....	235 00
C. S. Armstrong	Alton	359 80	....	359 80
A. D. Jack	Edwardsville	3,200 00	....	3,200 00
C. W. Seaman	Lebanon, German	900 00	5 00	905 00
David Dimond, D.D	Brighton	1,610 00	....	1,610 00
....	Belleville	1,565 00	....	1,565 00
Lyman Marshall	Lebanon	195 00	155 00	350 00
W. R. Adams	Shipman	20 00	10 00	30 00
....	Collinsville	....	100 00	100 00
W. L. Tarbet	Virden	477 00	392 00	869 00
Hugh Lamont	Carlinsville	5,000 00	....	5,000 00
E. W. Taylor	Walnut Grove	370 00	5 00	375 00
S. H. Hyde	Carrolton	830 25	5 00	835 25
S. A. Whitcomb	Hillsboro	2,500 00	....	2,500 00
T. E. Spilman	Butler	488 00	30 20	518 20
George Fraser	Greenville	1,450 00	....	1,450 00
A. S. Foster	Litchfield	275 00	....	275 00
John H. Reintz	Zion, German	....	34 00	34 00
W. H. Behle	St. John's, German	800 00	....	800 00
G. W. Fisher	Trenton	750 00	....	750 00
J. H. Spilman	Waveland	....	....	....
....	Whitehall	7,644 00	....	7,644 00
....	Lula	900 00	....	900 00
W. H. Templeton	Cave Spring	10 00	....	10 00
John Hood	Sparta	10,600 00	116 00	10,716 00
....	Denmark	200 00	....	200 00
R. G. Reynolds	Georgetown	....	5 00	5 00
		$45,465 55	$1,004 20	$46,469 75

Churches not reported, 21.

—o—

PRESBYTERY OF CAIRO.

Ministers.	Churches.	Home Objects.	General Objects.	Total.
P. S. Van Nest	New Duquoin	$1,069 00	....	$1,069 00
E. B. Olmstead	Caledonia	50 00	....	50 00
A. Johnston	Kinmundy	1,000 00	....	1,000 00
Joseph H. Scott	Metropolis	200 00	....	200 00
C. H. Foote	Cairo	2,600 00	....	2,600 00
E. F. Fish	Carbondale	....	$321 40	321 40
Edward Schofield	Centralia	870 00	155 00	1,025 00
John C. Wagaman	Nashville	1,500 00	....	1,500 00
I. N. Candee, D.D	Richview	135 00	....	135 00
George K. Perkins	Pinckneyville	....	4 50	4 50
George K. Perkins	Galum	....	1 10	1 10
S. Cook	Golconda	1,530 00	....	1,530 00

Continued on next page.

PRESBYTERY OF CAIRO.—CONTINUED.

Ministers.	Churches.	Home Objects.	General Objects.	Total.
John Huston	McLeansboro	400 00		400 00
	Olney	400 00		400 00
Thos. Smith	Richland		105 00	105 00
G. B. McComb	Equality	55 25		55 25
C. C. Hart	Shawneetown	600 00	420 00	1,020 00
G. C. Clark	Mt. Vernon	300 00		300 00
S. C. Baldridge	Friendsville		975 00	975 00
B. C. Swan	Carmis	292 00	10 00	302 00
Thos. Smith	Sharon		5 00	5 00
Thos. Smith	Enfield	1,811 00		1,811 00
R. C. Galbraith	Salem	100 00		100 00
Thos. Smith	Hermon		75 00	75 00
G. B. McComb	Harrisburg	25 00		25 00
	Saline Mines		10 00	10 00
	Wabash		184 00	184 00
R. G. Ross	Lawrenceville		15 00	15 00
R. G. Ross	Pisgah	598 00	70 00	668 00
R. G. Ross	Bridgeport		185 00	185 00
R. G. Ross	Union	139 00	42 00	181 00
R. C. Galbraith	Mt. Carmel		200 00	200 00
R. C. Galbraith	Flora	2,350 00		2,350 00
	Wakefield	820 00		820 00
		$16,844 25	$2,778 00	$19,622 25

Churches not reported, 20.

PRESBYTERY OF MATTOON.

Ministers.	Churches.	Home Objects.	General Objects.	Total.
R. M. Roberts	Arcola	$158 00		$158 00
Ellis Howell	Milton	1,850 00		1,850 00
	Pleasant Prairie	63 00	$10 00	73 00
	Paris	615 60	50 00	665 60
R. F. Patterson	Charleston	3,200 00		3,200 00
	Grandview	113 35	70 00	183 35
	Dudley	450 00		450 00
John Miller	New Hope	1,000 00		1,000 00
Thomas Spencer	Darwin	2,660 00		2,660 00
Thomas Spencer	York	551 00		551 00
Thos. M. Chestnut	Newton	83 00		83 00
R. A. Mitchell	Kansas	650 00	150 00	800 00
N. S. Dickey	Mattoon, First	1,029 30		1,029 30
	Mattoon, Second	120 00		120 00
	Palestine	220 00	25 00	245 00
	Beckwith Prairie	165 00		165 00
J. M. Johnson	Vandalia	3,624 50		3,624 50
Joseph Gordon	Vera	3 00		3 00
John Kidd	Pana	125 00		125 00
Robert Rudd	Taylorville	1,550 00		1,550 00
	Mowenqua	1,000 00		1,000 00
Edwin Black	Tuscola, First	1,200 00	45 00	1,245 00
	Tuscola, Second	1,700 00		1,700 00
R. D. Van Deursen	Shelbyville	1,476 00		1,476 00
W. B. Faris	Neoga	458 00		458 00
G. A. Pollock	Effingham	4,500 00		4,500 00
Nathaniel Williams	Prairie Bird	150 00		150 00
W. Maynard	Assumption	2,775 00		2,775 00
Clark Loudon	West Okaw	55 00		55 00
Charles F. Halsey	Cumberland	1,000 00		1,000 00
	Morrisonville	2,000 00		2,000 00
		$34,544 75	$350 00	$34,894 75

Churches not reported, 16.

SYNOD OF INDIANA NORTH.

PRESBYTERY OF FORT WAYNE.

Ministers.	Churches.	Home Objects.	General Objects.	Total.
W. M. Donaldson	Bluffton	$975 00		$975 00
W. J. Essick	Elkhart	6,000 00		6,000 00
Thomas H. Skinner, D.D.	Fort Wayne, First	3,500 00	$4,756 00	8,256 00
W. J. Erdman	Fort Wayne, Second	675 00		675 00
N. S. Smith	Fort Wayne, Third	1,017 00		1,017 00
T. E. Hughes	La Grange	1,400 00		1,400 00
W. M. Donaldson	New Lancaster	100 00	170 00	270 00
W. M. Donaldson	Pleasant Ridge	175 00	35 00	210 00
J. B. Fowler	Waterloo City	184 00		184 00
Theo. C. Jerome	Millersburg	200 00		200 00
J. H. L. Vannuys	Goshen		110 00	110 00
		$14,226 00	$5,071 00	$19,297 00

Churches not reported, 30.

—o—

PRESBYTERY OF LOGANSPORT.

Ministers.	Churches.	Home Objects.	General Objects.	Total.
L. M. Schofield	Logansport, First	$800 00	$1,000 00	$1,800 00
James Mathews, D.D.	Logansport, Second	520 00	740 00	1,260 00
W. C. Scofield	La Porte, Second	20,000 00		20,000 00
S. R. Seawright	Monticello	2,030 00		2,030 00
Walter Forsythe	South Bend	1,800 00		1,800 00
John B. Smith	Kentland	600 00	10 00	610 00
John Branch	Concord	20 00		20 00
John Branch	Indian Creek	20 00		20 00
John Branch	West Union	23 00		23 00
John Branch	Bethlehem	30 00		30 00
F. M. Elliott	Bethel	600 00		600 00
	Crown Point	85 00		85 00
Walter Pattinson	Rochester	1,100 00	50 00	1,150 00
L. Hughes	Remington	500 00		500 00
L. Hughes	Goodland	1,200 00		1,200 00
	Reynolds	238 00		238 00
E. H. Post	Lake Prairie	1,300 00		1,300 00
		$30,866 00	$1,800 00	$32,666 00

Churches not reported, 20.

PRESBYTERY OF CRAWFORDSVILLE.

Ministers.	Churches.	Home Objects.	General Objects.	Total.
Edward Barr	La Fayette, First	$22,800 00	$500 00	$23,300 00
Daniel Rice, D.D.	La Fayette, Second	4,125 00	5,530 00	9,655 00
J. A. Carnahan	Dayton	1,151 20	....	1,151 20
Luther Temple	West Point	40 00	....	40 00
W. W. Campbell	Delphi	600 00	....	600 00
Amos Jones	Rockfield	150 00	....	150 00
Amos Jones	Rock Creek	....	100 00	100 00
W. P. Koutz	Lexington	202 50	369 00	571 50
J. W. Torrence	Frankfort	1,018 00	16 68	1,034 68
John A. Campbell	Rossville	1,033 00	....	1,033 00
Joseph Platt	Sugar Creek	250 00	1,000 00	1,250 00
T. B. Adkins	Thorntown	1,580 00	150 00	1,730 00
J. Gilchrist	Bethel	245 00	....	245 00
R. B. Heron	Zionsville	....	20 00	20 00
F. M. Symmes	Hopewell	150 00	....	150 00
Robert F. Caldwell	Crawfordsville, First	1,500 00	....	1,500 00
John Safford	Crawfordsville (Centr'l)	165 00	2,805 00	2,970 00
Henry Clifton Thomson	Waveland	....	1,809 00	1,809 00
Wm. N. Steele	Parkersburg	615 00	....	615 00
John M. Bishop	Rockville	9,871 00	115 00	9,986 00
W. Y. Allen	Bethany	....	147 00	147 00
W. Y. Allen	Montezuma	25 00	....	25 00
J. Eastman	New Bethel	265 00	....	265 00
J. Hawks	Clinton	356 72	....	356 72
David M. Williamson	Perrysville	56 40	....	56 40
William Wilmer	Williamsport	110 00	....	110 00
J. Mitchell	West Lebanon	940 00	....	940 00
G. G. Mitchell	Attica	1,350 00	....	1,350 00
S. B. King	Rob Roy	150 00	....	150 00
S. B. King	Newtown	325 00	....	325 00
James Gilchrist	Dover	1,550 00	....	1,550 00
James Gilchrist	Darlington	2,100 00	....	2,100 00
		$52,723 82	$12,561 68	$65,285 50

Churches not reported, 15.

PRESBYTERY OF MUNCIE.

Ministers.	Churches.	Home Objects.	General Objects.	Total.
O. M. Todd	Muncie Union	$120 00	$144 00	$264 00
....	Tipton	125 00	....	125 00
D. M. Williamson	Perrysburg	1,200 00	181 25	1,381 25
A. S. Reid	Wabash	....	235 25	235 25
J. S. Craig	Noblesville	740 00	15 00	755 00
J. S. Craig	Boxley	....	40 00	40 00
W. Morris Grimes	Anderson	10,277 00	65 00	10,342 00
....	Marion	3,500 00	5 00	3,505 00
S. Wyckoff	Peru	4,092 00	....	4,092 00
John W. Drake	Union City	248 00	....	248 00
		$20,302 00	$685 50	$20,987 50

Churches not reported, 13.

SYNOD OF INDIANA SOUTH.

PRESBYTERY OF INDIANAPOLIS.

Ministers.	Churches.	Home Objects.	General Objects.	Total.
A. T. Moore	Bloomington, Walnut St	$1,021 00	$525 00	$1,546 00
R. D. Harper, D.D.	Indianapolis, First	33,422 45	1,317 00	34,739 45
Hanford A. Edson	Indianapolis, Second	13,547 00	305 00	13,852 00
Robt. Sloss	Indianapolis, Third	8,622 28	3,234 50	11,856 78
J. H. Morrow	Indianapolis, Fourth	5,000 00		5,000 00
W. B. Chamberlain	Indianapolis, Fifth	3,500 00		3,500 00
A. Parker	Columbus	2,900 00		2,900 00
Ambrose Dunn	Greenwood	546 50	11 43	557 93
S. E. Barr	Hopewell	5,125 00	171 69	5,296 69
A. C. Allen	Shiloh	73 80		73 80
E. W. Fisk, D.D.	Greencastle		36,750 00	36,750 00
Horace Bushnell, Jr.	Southport	50 00	407 17	457 17
	Acton	2,975 00		2,975 00
J. G. Williamson	Bethany	237 50	49 00	286 50
	Carpentersville	165 00	60 00	225 00
	New Pisgah	33 00	27 00	60 00
Geo. Long	Brownsburg	2,550 00		2,550 00
E. Thompson	New Hope		1,000 00	1,000 00
Geo. Long	Union	460 00		460 00
H. L. Dickenson	Edinburg	1,000 00	50 00	1,050 00
	St. Louis Crossing		10 00	10 00
J. Hawks	Putnamville	120 00	5 00	125 00
	Bainbridge		500 00	500 00
		$71,348 53	$45,422 79	$116,771 32

Churches not reported, 13.

—o—

PRESBYTERY OF WHITE WATER.

Ministers.	Churches.	Home Objects.	General Objects.	Total.
E. W. Thomson	Rushville	$3,250 00		$3,250 00
D. M. Stewart	Pleasant Grove		$131 00	131 00
L. B. W. Shryock	Knightstown	700 00		700 00
Eben Muse	Ebenezer		305 00	305 00
W. A. Patton	Cambridge City	250 00	18 00	268 00
	Providence	407 22	10 00	417 22
Eben Muse	Centreville	1,630 00		1,630 00
George O. Little	Conersville, First	215 00	530 00	745 00
J. C. Irwin	Greensburg	1,500 00		1,500 00
	Union	1,400 00		1,400 00
I. N. Hughes	Richmond	316 00		316 00
P. H. Golladay	Dunlapsville	220 00		220 00
A. L. Thomson	Mt. Carmel	11,500 00		11,500 00
Arthur T. Rankin	Clarksburg	2,644 00		2,644 00
Jas. H. Gill	Rising Sun	400 00		400 00
Jno. Sluter	Shelbyville, First	2,907 00		2,907 00
A. W. Freeman	Aurora	1,200 00		1,200 00
Eben Muse	Lewisville	1,220 00		1,220 00
J. H. Eschmeir	Shelbyville, Ger.	360 00		360 00
		$30,119 22	$994 00	$31,113 22

Churches not reported, 15.

PRESBYTERY OF NEW ALBANY.

Ministers.	Churches.	Home Objects.	General Objects.	Total.
Samuel Conn	New Albany, First	$3,700 00	$20,000 00	$23,700 00
Daniel Stewart, D.D.	New Albany, Second	2,300 00		2,300 00
Chas. Hutchinson	New Albany, Third	5,400 00		5,400 00
Josiah Crawford	New Washington		92 55	92 55
Josiah Crawford	Owen Creek	55 50	14 00	69 50
Thos. Whallon	Lexington	254 00	25 00	279 00
Joseph M. Hutchison	Jeffersonville	1,650 00	356 00	2,006 00
Philip Bevan	Leavenworth	271 50	225 00	496 50
Philip Bevan	Mt. Lebanon	1,200 00		1,200 00
Francis Xavier Kopf	Jackson Co. (German)	300 00	226 00	526 00
J. B. Crowe	Bedford	6,000 00		6,000 00
W. C. Young	Madison, First	1,170 00	1,145 00	2,315 00
Manuel J. Drennan	Madison, Second	1,700 00	1,700 00	3,400 00
Jas. A. McKee	North Vernon	1,747 00		1,747 00
I. I. St. John	Salem	840 00		840 00
Thos. A. Steele	Mitchell	7,000 00		7,000 00
Isaac B. Moore	Jefferson	94 00	6 00	100 00
	Hanover	2,595 00	600 00	3,195 00
	Seymour	72 00		72 00
M. D. A. Steen	Vevay		10 00	10 00
F. X. Kopf	Brownstown		100 00	100 00
J. M. McRee	Graham	710 00		710 00
Irvin I. St. John	Greenville		10 35	10 35
C. McCain	Monroe, Jefferson Co.	200 00		200 00
	New Philadelphia	52 25		52 25
C. K. Thompson	Oak Grove	815 00		815 00
R. C. McKinney	Orleans	139 25		139 20
Isaac B. Moore	Pleasant Top		65 00	65 00
John McCrae	Rehoboth	900 00		900 00
John McCrae	Sharon, Harrison Co.	50 00		50 00
Thos. Whallon	Sharon, Jefferson Co.	105 60		105 00
John McCrae	Utica	60 00		60 00
Jas. A. McKee	Vernon	400 00	25 00	425 00
	Zoar	170 00		170 00
John McCrae	Mt. Vernon		23 75	23 75
		$39,950 50	$24,623 65	$64,574 15

Churches not reported, 18.

—o—

PRESBYTERY OF VINCENNES.

Ministers.	Churches.	Home Objects.	General Objects.	Total.
T. S. Milligan	Bethany		$50 00	$50 00
T. S. Milligan	Bowling Green		15 00	15 00
Samuel B. Taggart	Brazil	$1,807 94		1,807 94
G. D. Parker	Bruceville	70 00		70 00
John P. Fox	Carlisle	1,700 00		1,700 00
T. S. Milligan	Poland	1,205 00		1,205 00
John Montgomery	Princeton	807 00	90 00	897 00
S. R. Alexander	Smyrna	1,560 00		1,560 00
L. R. Booth	Spencer	2,996 00		2,996 00
Samuel Ward	Claiborne		112 00	112 00
J. P. E. Kumler	Evansville, Walnut St.	600 00	1,147 00	1,747 00

Continued on next page.

PRESBYTERY OF VINCENNES.—CONTINUED.

Ministers.	Churches.	Home Objects.	General Objects.	Total.
C. B. H. Martin	Evansville, Vine St.	6,000 00		6,000 00
A. Taylor	Farmersburg		6 00	6 00
Thos. S. Milligan	Gosport		45 00	45 00
Samuel Ward	Howsville	1,022 00		1,022 00
Geo. D. Parker	Indiana, Upper	825 00		825 00
Augustus Taylor	Mt. Vernon	1,250 00		1,250 00
J. E. Lapsley	Terre Haute, First	3,200 00		3,200 00
Blackford Condit	Terre Haute, Second		1,250 00	1,250 00
Samuel Ward	Union		702 00	702 00
John F. Handy	Vincennes, First	3,000 00		3,000 00
Jos. Vance	Vincennes, Second	3,240 00		3,240 00
	Worthington	225 00	25 00	250 00
	Graysville	1,000 00		1,000 00
		$30,507 94	$3,442 00	$33,949 94

Churches not reported, 8.

SYNOD OF IOWA NORTH.

PRESBYTERY OF CEDAR RAPIDS.

Ministers.	Churches.	Home Objects.	General Objects.	Total.
James Knox	Cedar Rapids, First	$8,002 55	$600 00	$8,602 55
A. N. Keigwin	Cedar Rapids, Second	3,873 63	28 02	3,901 65
Alex. S. Marshall	Marion	363 00	300 50	663 50
N. C. Robinson	Vinton, First	1,000 00	600 00	1,600 00
J. W. Crawford	Vinton, Second	600 00	400 00	1,000 00
Hannibal L. Stanley	Wheatland	571 64		571 64
Jas. L. Wilson	Scotch Grove		140 00	140 00
John Gilmore	Andrew	150 00		150 00
J. N. Wilson	Wayne		50 00	50 00
J. N. Wilson	Anamosa	415 00	15 00	430 00
Alex. Caldwell	Central Shellsburg	100 00		100 00
A. G. Martyn	Shellsburg	1,275 00		1,275 00
A. G. Martyn	Pleasant Hill	75 00		75 00
H. K. Hennigly	Linn Grove	1,958 00		1,958 00
		$18,383 82	$2,133 52	$20,517 34

Churches not reported, 18.

PRESBYTERY OF DUBUQUE.

Ministers.	Churches.	Home Objects.	General Objects.	Total.
Alvah Day	Manchester		$25 00	$25 00
J. J. Weiss	McGregor		6 00	6 00
Alvah Day	Liberty		11 00	11 00
Alvah Day	Byron Centre		32 57	32 57
	Waukon		37 35	37 35
John G. Schaible	Independence, German	$78 00		78 00
J. D. Caldwell	Pleasant Grove	480 00		480 00
S. G. Spees, D.D	Dubuque, Second	3,901 57		3,901 57
J. M. Boggs	Jesup		355 00	355 00
James W. Dickey	Bethel, West Union	2,663 00		2,663 00
James Frothingham	Lansing, First	150 00	60 00	210 00
Merit Harmon	Prairie		11 00	11 00
Samuel Hodge	Hopkinton		2,490 00	2,490 00
T. S. Bailey	Epworth	150 00	30 00	180 00
T. S. Bailey	Peosta		30 00	30 00
T. S. Bailey	Farley	1,600 00		1,600 00
	Mt. Hope	1,200 00		1,200 00
		$10,222 57	$3,087 92	$13,310 49

Churches not reported, 18.

———o———

PRESBYTERY OF WATERLOO.

Ministers.	Churches.	Home Objects.	General Objects.	Total.
W. W. Thorpe	Waterloo	$1,600 00		$1,600 00
Luther Dodd	Salem		$50 00	50 00
Charles R. French	Grundy Centre	362 00		362 00
Benjamin Mills	Ackley	419 75		419 75
A. B. Goodale	Marshaltown	1,800 00	290 00	2,090 00
Isaiah Reid	Nevada	175 00		175 00
D. Blakely	Steamboat Rock	50 00		50 00
Stephen Phelps	Cedar Valley	1,500 00		1,500 00
James A. Hoyt	Big Creek	75 00		75 00
S. R. Griffiths	Cedar Falls	1,200 00		1.200 00
C. S. Marvin	Floyd	4,200 00		4,200 00
Geo. T. Everest	Northwood	827 00		827 00
		$12,208 75	$340 00	$12,548 75

Churches not reported, 18.

PRESBYTERY OF FORT DODGE.

Ministers.	Churches.	Home Objects.	General Objects.	Total.
J. M. Phillips............	Fort Dodge...........	$150 00	....	$150 00
J. S. Dunning	Jefferson.............	230 00	....	230 00
E. H. Avery.............	Sioux City............	1,425 00	....	1,425 00
		$1,805 00	....	$1,805 00

Churches not reported, 11

SYNOD OF IOWA SOUTH.

PRESBYTERY OF DES MOINES.

Ministers.	Churches.	Home Objects.	General Objects.	Total.
....	Afton.................	$512 00	....	$512 00
J. M. Batchelder..........	Albia.................	3,840 00	....	3,840 00
G. W. Jenks........... ..	Centreville...........	125 00	....	125 00
A. A. Dinsmore...........	Des Moines, First......	....	$4,746 50	4,746 50
Thomas O. Rice...........	Des Moines, Central...	....	23,800 00	23,800 00
J. D. Jones..............	Columbia.............	150 00	....	150 00
A. A. Mathes.............	Decatur City..........	....	130 00	130 00
Wm. Campbell............	De Soto..............	1,212 00	....	1,212 00
B. O. Junkin	Dexter...............	1,340 00	....	1,340 00
Wm. Campbell............	Earlham..............	2,048 00	....	2,048 00
C. R. Van Emen..........	Garden Grove.........	75 00	....	75 00
....	Guthrie..............	100 00	....	100 00
Silas Johnson............	Indianola.............	3,000 00	....	3,000 00
P. H. Jacob..............	Knoxville.............	250 00	10 00	260 00
A. A. Mathes.............	Leon.................	1,500 00	....	1,500 00
Wm. Kendrick............	Moulton..............	1,400 00	....	1,400 00
John Fisher	Olivet	130 00	13 00	143 00
J. Osmond...............	Osceola..............	910 00	....	910 00
S. C. McCune.............	Oskaloolsa	238 00	....	238 00
John Fisher,.............	Pella.................	800 00	....	800 00
J. D. Jones..............	Plymouth.............	1,350 00	....	1,350 00
....	Russell...............	81 00	....	81 00
....	Unionville	268 00	....	268 00
J. H. Potter..............	Wintersett............	115 00	....	115 00
S. W. Elliott.............	Woodburn....	600 00	....	600 00
		$20,044 00	$28,699 50	$48,743 50

Churches not reported, 20.

PRESBYTERY OF IOWA

Ministers.	Churches.	Home Objects.	General Objects.	Total.
David S. Tappan	Mt. Pleasant, First	$1,600 00	....	$1,600 00
Thos. McClelland	Winfield	299 00	....	299 00
Alex. Scott	Kossuth	858 00	....	858 00
D. Brown	Kirkville	205 00	....	205 00
Jas. Stewart Reed	Eddyville	102 00	....	102 00
Carson Reed	Fairfield	358 50	$15 00	373 50
H. R. Lewis	Bonaparte	1,600 00	....	1,600 00
H. R. Lewis	Little Cedar	800 00	....	800 00
Wm. Reed	Bentonsport	500 00	....	500 00
J. G. Condit	Libertyville	217 00	....	217 00
S. R. Bellville	Montrose	1,200 00	....	1,200 00
H. B. Knight	Ottumwa	25 00	30 00	55 00
J. M. McElroy	Batavia	250 00	....	250 00
John Glass	Toolsboro	2,000 00	....	2,000 00
G. C. Beamen	Croton	225 00	....	225 00
		$10,229 50	$45 00	$10,284 50

Churches not reported, 33.

—o—

PRESBYTERY OF IOWA CITY.

Ministers.	Churches.	Home Objects.	General Objects.	Total.
S. M. Osmond	Iowa City	$3,592 50	$210 00	$3,802 50
A. R. Mathes	Wilton	947 50	....	947 50
J. W. Knott	Mechanicsville	....	73 50	73 50
J. D. Mason	Long Grove	1,000 00	....	1,000 00
T. D. Wallace	Washington	72 00	50 00	122 00
D. V. Smock	Lafayette	70 00	5 00	75 00
Edwin C. Haskell	Brooklyn	450 00	....	450 00
H. H. Kellogg, Jr	Victor	1,400 00	....	1,400 00
H. H. Kellogg	Ladora	1,000 00	....	1,000 00
Wm. Young	Deep River	200 00	....	200 00
J. B. Stewart	Davenport	1,100 00	2,000 00	3,100 00
J. B. McBride	Princeton	....	10 00	10 00
A. R. Mathes	Sugar Creek	....	146 50	146 50
J. S. Dickey	Red Oak	....	21 00	21 00
C. P. Spinning	Fair View	55 00	15 00	70 00
J. D. Mason	Summit	....	50 00	50 00
R. W. Haines	Crawfordsville	....	45 00	45 00
J. Wilson	Marengo	100 00	....	100 00
R. R. Court	Malcolm	964 50	....	964 50
Jos. M. Wilson	Columbus City	300 00	....	300 00
George Earhart	Oxford	700 00	....	700 00
		$11,951 50	$2,626 00	$14,577 50

Churches not reported, 29.

PRESBYTERY OF MISSOURI RIVER.

Ministers.	Churches.	Home Objects.	General Objects.	Total.
	Sidney, Iowa	$5,720 21		$5,720 21
A. F. Randolph	Bedford	825 00		825 00
T. H. Cleland, Jr	Council Bluff	1,713 65	$325 00	2,038 65
R. R. Westcott	Clarinda	125 00		125 00
	Glenwood	200 00		200 00
G. G. Ferguson	Hamburgh	2,000 00		2,000 00
Wm. Pilan	Missouri Valley	2,000 00		2,000 00
T. K. Hodges	Logan		65 00	65 00
M. Hughes	Atlantic	1,350 00		1,350 00
T. K. Hodges	Hazeldell	800 00		800 00
M. Hughes	Avoca	1,460 00		1,460 00
W. Hamilton	Blackbird Hills, Neb		50 00	50 00
J. D. Kerr	Nebraska City	1,200 00		1,200 00
D. W. Cameron	Plattsmouth	650 00		650 00
W. H. Clark, S.S	Ponca	1,000 00		1,000 00
A. L. Payson	Bellvue	250 00		250 00
H. P. Peck	Lincoln	2,600 00		2,600 00
George D. Stewart	Omaha, Second	1,100 00		1,100 00
Jos. M, Wilson	Seward	600 00		600 00
John M. Peebles	Decatur	919 00		919 00
John M. Peebles	Lyons	611 50		611 50
B. F. McNeil	Beatrice	1,800 00		1,800 00
A. T. Wood	Helena	500 00		500 00
J. B. Long	Tekamah	836 00	5 00	841 00
Jos. M. Wilson	Madison	100 00		100 00
Robt. Burgess	Woodbine		5 00	5 00
J. B. Long	Bell Creek	555 00		555 00
		$28,915 36	$450 00	$29,365 36

Churches not reported, 20.

SYNOD OF KANSAS.

PRESBYTERY OF EMPORIA.

Ministers.	Churches.	Home Objects.	General Objects.	Total.
N. A. Rankin	Burlingame	$180 00		$180 00
J. S. Sherrill	Quenemo	2,035 00	$242 40	2,277 40
Albert McCalla	Emporia	4,700 00		4,700 00
James Gordon	Eldorado	600 00		600 00
W. K. Boggs	Wichita	500 00		500 00
W. W. Curtis	Lyndon	500 00		500 00
W. W. Curtis	Osage City	50 00		50 00
		$8,565 00	$242 40	$8,807 40

Churches not reported, 4.

PRESBYTERY OF HIGHLAND.

Ministers.	Churches.	Home Objects.	General Objects.	Total.
A. S. McConnell	Highland		$2,345 00	$2,345 00
	Troy	$1,200 00		1,200 00
D. D. Green	Doniphan	503 00		503 00
Edward Cooper	Atchison	500 00		500 00
Geo. F. Chapin	Irving	450 00	3,025 00	3,475 00
W. G. Thomas	Washington	600 00		600 00
H. E. Morrell	Neuchatel	1,200 00		1,200 00
D. R. Todd	Netawaka	500 00		500 00
D. R. Todd	Kennekuk	3 50		3 50
Geo. F. Chapin	Spring Side		300 00	300 00
A. H. Libby	Maryville	1,200 00		1,200 00
	Eureka		15 00	15 00
		$6,156 50	$5,685 00	$11,841 50

Churches not reported, 6.

———o———

PRESBYTERY OF TOPEKA.

Ministers.	Churches.	Home Objects.	General Objects.	Total.
J. G. Reaser, D.D.	Leavenworth, Westm'r	$14,425 00		$14,425 00
Eben Blackly	Quindaro		$300 00	
J. N. Rankin	Olathe	280 00		280 00
	Gardner	1,318 00		1,318 00
J. N. Rankin	Spring Hill	1,952 00		1,952 00
V. M. King	Black Jack	300 00	30 00	330 00
V. M. King	Baldwin City	130 00	27 00	157 00
V. M. King	Vineland		5 00	5 00
H. Stout	Clinton	160 00	123 00	283 00
	Lawrence	1,500 00		1,500 00
Geo. A. Irvin	Oskaloosa	1,900 00		1,900 00
Geo. A. Irvin	Perryville	728 00		728 00
Francis S. McCabe	Topeka	715 00		715 00
John Mack	Auburn	570 00		570 00
I. T. Whittemore	Wamego	1,864 50		1,864 50
Joseph H. Reid	Manhattan	5,000 00		5,000 00
John A. Anderson	Junction City	10,149 00		10,149 00
		$40,991 50	$485 00	$41,476 50

Churches not reported, 19.

PRESBYTERY OF NEOSHO.

Ministers.	Churches.	Home Objects.	General Objects.	Total.
....	Montana..............	$245 00	....	$245 00
T. Y. Gardner............	Fort Scott............	405 00	....	405 00
H. W. Stratton	Iola...................	....	$65 00	65 00
S. T. McClure.............	Girard................	3,000 00	....	3,000 00
E. K. Lynn..............	Scipio................	....	5 00	5 00
G. W. McMillen...........	New Chicago..........	400 00	....	400 00
John Elliot................	Ottawa...............	970 00	....	970 00
Ira S. Dodd..............	Garnet................	50 00	10 00	60 00
H. D. Lougheed...........	Neo de Sha...........	3,023 00	....	3,023 00
H. H. Cambern...........	La Dore..............	....	10 00	10 00
W. S. Robertson..........	Creek Mission.........	20 00	....	20 00
D. V. Mayo..............	Paola.................	2,184 00	....	2,184 00
		$10,297 00	$90 00	$10,387 00

Churches not reported, 32.

SYNOD OF KENTUCKY.

PRESBYTERY OF EBENEZER.

Ministers.	Churches.	Home Objects.	General Objects.	Total.
John H. Nesbit...........	Frankfort.............	....	$175 00	$175 00
....	Mt. Sterling..........	....	5 00	5 00
....	Mt. Horeb.............	....	75 00	75 00
W. C. Condit............	Ashland..............	$842 73	....	842 73
J. M. Worrall, D.D.......	Covington, First......	40,000 00	96 00	40,096 00
....	Moorefield............	....	20 00	20 00
....	Sharpsburg...........	140 00	....	140 00
G. M. McCampbell........	Maysville.............	440 70	10 00	450 70
....	Falmouth.............	....	93 00	93 00
....	Murphyville..........	....	28 00	28 00
G. W. F. Birch...........	Lexington, Second....	300 00	8,236 50	8,536 50
James P. Hendrick........	Flemingsburg.........	....	600 00	600 00
....	Newport, First........	1,200 00	....	1,200 00
Fauntleroy Senour........	Newport, Second......	3,000 00	....	3,000 00
....	Burlington...........	....	10 00	10 00
		$45,923 43	$9,348 50	$55,271 93

Churches not reported, 20.

PRESBYTERY OF LOUISVILLE.

Ministers.	Churches.	Home Objects.	General Objects.	Total.
....	Shelbyville...........	$1,355 00	....	$1,355 00
....	Olivet...............	2,700 00	$59 00	2,759 00
James H. Dinsmore.......	Hopkinsville..........	....	225 00	225 00
E. P. Humphrey, D.D.....	Louisville, College St..	4,000 00	3,107 00	7,107 00
....	Louisville, Chestnut St.	....	239 00	239 00
J. S. Hays, D.D..........	Louisville, Walnut St..	420 00	250 00	670 00
W. C. Matthews, D.D.....	Louisville, Fourth.....	....	500 00	500 00
A. C. Dickerson..........	Caney Fork..........	....	30 00	30 00
		$8,475 00	$4,410 00	$12,885 00

Churches not reported, 26.

——o——

PRESBYTERY OF TRANSYLVANIA.

Ministers.	Churches.	Home Objects.	General Objects.	Total.
S. S. McRoberts..........	Stanford.............	....	$53 00	$53 00
....	Danville, Second......	$3,400 00	270 00	3,670 00
Thomas M. Gunn.........	Munfordsville.........	100 00	110 00	210 00
....	Harrodsburg..........	....	45 00	45 00
....	Lancaster............	....	22 00	22 00
....	Bethel Union..........	2,000 00	....	2,000 00
James P. McMillan........	Burkesville...........	....	16 00	16 00
....	Concord, Col'd........	337 85	....	337 85
Thomas M. Gunn.........	Edmonton...........	300 00	....	300 00
		$6,137 85	$516 00	$6,653 85

Churches not reported, 16.

SYNOD OF LONG ISLAND.

PRESBYTERY OF BROOKLYN.

Ministers.	Churches.	Home Objects.	General Objects.	Total.
J. D. Wells, D.D.	Brooklyn, South 3d St.	$13,235 57	....	$13,235 57
Adam McClelland	Brooklyn, Lawrence St.	443 00	....	443 00
A. N. Freeman	Brooklyn, Siloam	....	$100 00	100 00
Chas. S. Pomeroy	Brooklyn, Ross St.	36,750 00	....	36,750 00
Theo. L. Cuyler, D.D.	Brooklyn, Lafayette Av.	13,432 00	756 00	14,188 00
T. De Witt Talmage	Brooklyn, Central	17,000 00	....	17,000 00
Norman Seaver, D.D	Brooklyn, First	15,000 00	2,000 00	17,000 00
Wm. H. Taylor	Greenpoint	7,000 00	....	7,000 00
J. E. Rockwell, D.D.	Edgewater, S. I.	3,135 00	500 00	3,635 00
J. G. Butler, D.D.	Brooklyn, First, E. D.	....	185 00	185 00
Alex. B. Lamberton	Tompkins Ave.	....	295 00	295 00
		$105,995 57	$3,836 00	$109,831 57

Churches not reported, 12.

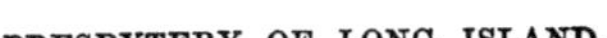

PRESBYTERY OF LONG ISLAND.

Ministers.	Churches.	Home Objects.	General Objects.	Total.
Thos. Harries	Shelter Island	$712 00	....	$712 00
J. T. Hamlin	Mattituck	2,500 00	....	2,500 00
Epher Whitaker	Southold	1,550 00	....	1,550 00
Chas. Sturgis	Middletown	1,142 00	$35 00	1,177 00
Robt. Scott	Moriches	100 00	....	100 00
W. G. Barnes	Sag Harbor	3,000 00	....	3,000 00
Wm. H. Littell	Setauket	1,400 00	....	1,400 00
A. Shiland	South Hampton	111 22	268 99	380 21
Edward Stratton	Port Jefferson, First Ch.	900 00	....	900 00
		$11,415 22	$303 99	$11,719 21

Churches not reported, 14.

PRESBYTERY OF NASSAU.

Ministers.	Churches.	Home Objects.	General Objects.	Total.
John P. Knox	Newtown	$610 00	....	$610 00
B. F. Stead, D.D.	Astoria	3,100 00	$1,000 00	4,100 00
Marcus Burr	Freeport	500 00	....	500 00
Benj. L. Swan	Oyster Bay	1,073 00	....	1,073 00
Jas. B. Finch	Hempstead	1,872 00	....	1,872 00
Alex. Miller	Springfield, First Ch.	1,175 00	70 00	1,245 00
Sidney G. Law	Fresh Pond	4,000 00	....	4,000 00
Samuel L. Carter	Huntington, First	1,300 00	200 00	1,500 00
Wm. W. Knox	Huntington, Second	5,285 00	....	5,285 00
Lewis Lampman	Jamaica	761 00	387 00	1,148 00
J. M. Huntting, Jr.	Sweet Hollow	99 72	....	99 72
John Murdoch	Islip	2,375 00	....	2,375 00
		$22,150 72	$1,608 00	$23,808 72

Churches not reported, 9.

SYNOD OF MICHIGAN.

PRESBYTERY OF DETROIT.

Ministers.	Churches.	Home Objects.	General Objects.	Total.
W. Hogarth, D.D.	Detroit, Jefferson Ave.	....	$2,280 00	$2,280 00
W. A. McCorkle	Detroit, First	....	7,697 50	7,697 50
W. E. McLaren	Detroit, Westminster	$1,817 35	....	1,817 35
A. T. Pierson	Detroit, Fort St.	34,000 00	1,339 25	35,339 25
Norman Kellogg	Stony Creek	....	157 00	157 00
L. Chandler	White Lake	2,200 00	....	2,200 00
H. N. Bissell	Mt. Clemens	521 00	....	521 00
G. L. Foster	Howell	500 00	....	500 00
J. S. Smith	Southfield	442 38	....	442 38
Geo. P. Tindall	Ypsilanti	752 40	684 00	1,436 40
A. E. Hastings	Birmingham, First	200 00	15 00	215 00
Edward Dickinson	Holly	100 00	154 00	254 00
....	Ann Arbor	2,000 00	....	2,000 00
W. J. Parrot	Pontiac	15,500 00	....	15,500 00
A. W. Sanford	Wyandotte	1,450 00	....	1,450 00
....	Erin	43 00	....	43 00
J. S. Lord, S. S.	Springfield	626 00	....	626 00
J. S. Lord, S. S.	Independence	47 00	....	47 00
....	Plymouth, Second	....	....	....
		$60,199 13	$12,326 75	$72,525 88

Churches not reported, 14.

PRESBYTERY OF GRAND RAPIDS.

Ministers.	Churches.	Home Objects.	General Objects.	Total.
Jonas Denton	Greenwood	....	$11 84	$11 84
J. Walker	Pewamo	$1,608 05	75 00	1,683 05
R. S. Goodman	Westminster, G'd Rp'ds	610 00	6 00	616 00
J. Pierson	Ionia	4,000 00	....	4,000 00
J. M. Cross, D.D	Grand Haven	807 00	....	807 00
Aug. Marsh	Portland	126 44	130 00	256 44
Geo. Ransom	Muir	60 00	8 00	68 00
J. N. Diament	Stanton	100 00	....	100 00
....	Manistee	776 00	....	776 00
A. G. Beebe	Spring Lake	3,121 64	....	3,121 64
Wm. U. Benedict	Sebewa	30 00	....	30 00
H. H. Northrup	Grand Rapids, First	364 00	....	364 00
L. M. Birge	Ada	1,700 00	....	1,700 00
R. F. Murden	Montague	51 62	25 00	76 62
John Arends	Zealand	....	10 00	10 00
I. B. Hall	East Bay	15 00	....	15 00
		$13,369 75	$265 84	$13,635 59

Churches not reported, 5.

—o—

PRESBYTERY OF KALAMAZOO.

Ministers.	Churches.	Home Objects.	General Objects.	Total.
Milton Bradley	Richland	$708 53	$359 50	$1,068 03
John Sailor	Allegan	1,526 00	....	1,526 00
P. A. McMartin	Plainwell	2,400 00	....	2,400 00
J. W. McGregor	Schoolcraft	50 00	....	50 00
Joseph A. Ramsey	Three Rivers	1,400 00	100 00	1,500 00
C. M. Temple	Sturgis	270 00	30 00	300 00
John V. Hilton	Kalamazoo	....	3,810 00	3,810 00
Joseph A. Ranney	Parkville	....	100 00	100 00
		$6,411 53	$4,342 50	$10,754 03

Churches not reported, 11.

PRESBYTERY OF LANSING.

Ministers.	Churches.	Home Objects.	General Objects.	Total.
John Gerrish	Homer		$380 00	$380 00
Thos. Sherrard	Brooklyn	$418 00		418 00
D. M. Cooper	Albion	990 00	10 00	1,000 00
Archd. Shaw	Concord	332 00	505 00	837 00
Geo. W. Barlow	Mason, First Pres.		128 50	128 50
Theo. D. Marsh	Hastings	103 00	15 00	118 00
	Lansing, First	125 00		125 00
	Okemos	225 00		225 00
Francis M. Wood	Marshall	132 00	734 00	866 00
	Dansville		16 00	16 00
Alfred Bryant	Lansing, Franklin St.	869 00		869 00
Wm. U. Benedict	Sunfield		25 00	25 00
		$3,194 00	$1,813 50	$4,907 50

Churches not reported, 13.

—o—

PRESBYTERY OF MONROE.

Ministers.	Churches.	Home Objects.	General Objects.	Total.
A. Scofield	California	$1,500 00		$1,500 00
C. N. Mattoon, D.D.	Hudson	2,200 00		2,200 00
W. S. Taylor	Petersburg	600 00		600 00
W. S. Taylor	Deerfield	250 00		250 00
W. H. Webb	Adrian	5,698 00		5,698 00
W. J. Stoutenburgh	Tecumseh	3,432 00	48 00	3,480 00
W. C. Porter	Coldwater	4,484 08		4,484 08
W. W. Newell, Jr.	Monroe	2,684 10	45 00	2,729 10
V. A. Lewis	Hillsdale	70 00		70 00
E. F. Tanner	La Salle	220 00		220 00
	Ida	1,000 00		1,000 00
Geo. B. Barnes	Quincy, First Ch.	1,505 00		1,505 00
	Erie	2,000 00		2,000 00
John W. Baynes	Blissfield	150 00		150 00
	Palmyra	47 70		47 70
L. B. Pert	Raisin	1,837 00		1,837 00
Jas. Quick	Reading	1,550 00		1,550 00
	Clayton	85 59		85 59
T. L. Waldo	Manchester	72 00	18 00	90 00
		$29,385 47	$111 00	$29,496 47

Churches not reported, 6.

PRESBYTERY OF SAGINAW.

Ministers.	Churches.	Home Objects.	General Objects.	Total.
....	Byron	$44 00	....	$44 00
J. A. Wight..............	Bay City..............	1,344 00	$183 00	1,527 00
E. F. Waldo..............	Tawas City	550 00	....	550 00
S. Ellis Wishard..........	East Saginaw.........	585 00	100 00	685 00
Geo. Duffield, D.D........	Saginaw City, 1st Pres.	3,585 16	....	3,585 16
Wm. G. Smith............	Woodhull.............	750 00	....	750 00
J. L. Willett..............	Pine River............	175 00	....	175 00
J. L. Willett..............	Lafayette and Emerson	100 00	5 00	105 00
....	Midland City..........	400 00	....	400 00
....	Bennington...........	....	13 00	13 00
....	Corunna..............	....	20 00	20 00
E. F. Waldo..............	East Tawas...........	865 00	....	865 00
....	Saginaw..............	....	50 00	50 00
		$8,398 16	$371 00	$8,769 16

Churches not reported, 27.

SYNOD OF MINNESOTA.

PRESBYTERY OF MANKATO.

Ministers.	Churches.	Home Objects.	General Objects.	Total.
Joseph B. Little...........	Mankato	$2,100 00	$176 00	$2,276 00
A. H. Kerr................	St. Peters.............	8,242 00	42 00	8,284 00
S. D. Westfall.............	Redwood Falls........	1,000 00	....	1,000 00
R. McQuesten.............	Le Sueur.............	500 00	....	500 00
A. P. Bissell..............	Blue Earth City.......	1,800 00	....	1,800 00
Edward Savage...........	Jackson	....	10 00	10 00
D. J. Lewis...............	South Bend...........	....	14 50	14 50
D. J. Lewis...............	Judson	750 00	....	750 00
....	Winnebago Agency....	....	....	....
S. D. Westfall............	Beaver Falls..........	410 00	....	410 00
Christian Wisner..........	Madelia..............	850 00	....	850 00
....	Lake Crystal..........	825 00	....	825 00
T. B. Haskell.............	Winnebago City.......	4,434 00	....	4,434 00
J. J. Ward...............	Wells................	2,000 00	....	2,000 00
....	Yellow Medecine......	300 00	....	300 00
....	Eden................	550 00	....	550 00
		$23,761 00	$242 50	$24,003 50

Churches not reported, 10.

PRESBYTERY OF ST. PAUL.

Ministers.	Churches.	Home Objects.	General Objects.	Total.
G. H. Pond	Oak Grove	$95 00	$95 00	$190 00
J. W. Hancock	Florence	1,155 00	....	1,155 00
J. W. Hancock	Goodhue	1,300 00	....	1,300 00
J. Mattocks	St. Paul, First	5,000 00	50 00	5,050 00
James H. Hunter	Dundas	151 00	4 00	155 00
....	White Bear Lake	405 00		405 00
E. V. Campbell	St. Cloud	115 00	....	354 51
R. F. Sample	Westminster, Minneap's	5,671 50	1,340 00	6,772 00
J. Q. Hall	Taylor's Falls	100 00	100 00	200 00
F. T. Brown, D.D	St. Paul, Central	8,000 00	500 00	8,500 00
Daniel B. Jackson	Litchfield and Kingston	500 00	....	500 00
Edward B. Wright	Stillwater, First	1,232 00	100 00	1,332 00
J. E. Miller	Shakopee	....	30 00	30 00
....	Minneapolis, First	1,000 00	58 60	1,058 60
D. E. Wells	Redwing	2,000 00	170 00	2,170 00
Oscar H. Elmar	Sank Centre	75 00	....	75 00
I. C. Sloan	Belle Plaine	964 00	10 00	974 00
....	Farmington	250 00	....	250 00
David R. Breed	House of Hope	12,178 00	1,070 00	13,248 00
J. A. McGowan	Wilmar, First	315 00	....	315 00
J. W. Hancock	West Florence	1,155 00	5 00	1,160 00
Chas. Thayer	Long Lake	800 00	....	800 00
Chas. Thayer	Delano	700 00	....	700 00
Chas. Thayer	Rockford	150 00	....	150 00
Isaac Watts Monfort	St. Anthony	2,220 00	86 00	2.308 00
Hugh Wallace Todd	Lake City	325 00	....	325 00
J. Cochran	Stillwater, Second	380 00	....	380 00
....	Pine City	200 00	....	200 00
....	Duluth	11,686 50	....	11.686 50
J. Q. Hall	St. Croix Falls	747 00		747 00
		$58,870 01	$3,618 00	$62,188 61

Churches not reported, 11.

——o——

PRESBYTERY OF WINONA.

Ministers.	Churches.	Home Objects.	General Objects.	Total.
J. T. Killen	Rochester	$1,132 00	....	$1,132 00
J. A. Laurie	Le Roy	396 00	....	396 00
Thomas Burnett	Orinoco	852 00	....	852 00
J. M. Brack	Sheldon	150 00	....	150 00
....	Winona (German)	40 00	....	40 00
J. L. Howell	Chatfield	65 00	....	65 00
Geo. Ainslie	Stewartsville	1,200 00	....	1,200 00
Geo. Ainslie	Chester	32 85	....	32 85
Geo. Ainslie	Dresser Valley	32 85	....	32 85
Silas Hazlett	Harmony	250 00	....	250 00
D. L. Kiehle	Preston	225 00	....	225 00
....	Austin	....	10 00	10 00
W. S. Wilson	Owatonna	588 00	....	588 00
R. H. Cunningham	Rushford	....	15 00	15 00
R. H. Cunningham	Fremont	450 00	20 00	470 00
R. B. Abbott	Albert Lea	275 00	....	275 00
J. M. McNulty	Winona	500 00	....	500 00
Geo. Ainslie	Washington	1,400 00	....	1,400 00
....	Houston	200 00	....	200 00
J. L. Merritt	St. Charles	593 00	5 00	598 00
A. Busch	Frank Hill	30 00	....	30 00
		$8.411 70	$50 00	$8,461 70

Churches not reported, 17.

SYNOD OF MISSOURI.

PRESBYTERY OF OSAGE.

Ministers.	Churches.	Home Objects.	General Objects.	Total.
R. Irwin	Kansas City, First	$150 00		$150 00
J. H. Byers	Kansas City, Third	500 00		500 00
J. T. Lapsley	Pleasant Hill	900 00		900 00
	Knob Noster	400 00		400 00
J. H. Clark	Warrensburg	4,000 00		4,000 00
J. W. Clark	Lexington	1,750 00		1,750 00
James Young	High Point	700 00		700 00
	La Monte	1,000 00		1,000 00
D. McNaughton	Morristown	800 00		800 00
S. G. Clark	Hudson	700 00	220 00	920 00
D. C. Milner	Osceola	500 00		500 00
J. B. Allen	Clinton	277 00		277 00
J. Addison Whitaker	Jefferson City	54 60	15 00	69 60
Benj. F. Powelson	Deep Water	400 00		400 00
Benj. F. Powelson	Montrose	335 00		335 00
		$12,466 60	$235 00	$12,701 60

Churches not reported, 23.

PRESBYTERY OF OZARK.

Ministers.	Churches.	Home Objects.	General Objects.	Total.
James A. Paige	Calvary	$1,699 55		$1,699 55
Wm. Pinkerton	Carthage	4,000 00		4,000 00
J. M. Brown	Neosho	1,300 00		1,300 00
	Springfield	1,700 00		1,700 00
L. J. Matthews	Peace Valley	310 00		310 00
E. M. Halbert	Mt. Zion	200 00		200 00
W. R. Fulton	Greenfield (Ebenezer)	500 00		500 00
A. W. Elliott	Conway	200 00		200 00
	Ozark Prairie	4,000 00		4,000 00
		$13,909 55		$13,909 55

Churches not reported, 10.

PRESBYTERY OF PALMYRA.

Ministers.	Churches.	Home Objects.	General Objects.	Total.
John Leighton............	Hannibal, First.......	$5,500 00	....	$5,500 00
J. P. Finley..............	Brookfield, First......	3,790 00	....	3,790 00
D. R. Hindman...........	Memphis.............	110 00	....	110 00
James S. Boyd............	Kirksville.............	359 00	....	359 00
....	Grantsville...........	600 00	....	600 00
James A. Darrah..........	West Ely.............	260 00	....	260 00
Thomas H. Tatlow........	Newark..............	150 00	....	150 00
J. J. Wilson...............	Pleasant Prairie.......	70 00	....	70 00
G. F. Davis...............	La Grange............	75 00	....	75 00
William P. Cochran.......	Palmyra..............	260 00	$26 00	286 00
W. P. Teitsworth..........	Clark City............	....	20,000 00	20,000 00
John T. Evans............	Welch (B'ds-EyeRidge)	115 00	....	115 00
		$11,289 00	$20,026 00	$31,315 00

Churches not reported, 18.

—o—

PRESBYTERY OF PLATTE.

Ministers.	Churches.	Home Objects.	General Objects.	Total.
J. M. Green..............	Cameron	$2,000 00	....	$2,000 00
J. N. Young..............	Fillmore..............	100 00	....	100 00
....	Lathrop	2,000 00	$5 00	2,005 00
Joel Kennedy.............	Hamilton.............	1,500 00	....	1,500 00
N. H. Smith..............	Albany	125 00	10 00	135 00
Elisha B. Sherwood........	Dawn	1,300 00	....	1,300 00
E. B. Sherwood...........	Willow Brook.........	900 00	....	900 00
J. S. Reeves..............	Platte City............	200 00	....	200 00
H. Bullard................	Westminster, St. Joseph	3,374 00	....	3,374 00
J. M. Green	Easton................	500 00	....	500 00
N. H. Smith..............	Mt. Zion..............	50 00	....	50 00
J. M. Crawford...........	Maryville.............	2,500 00	....	2,500 00
E. B. Sherwood...........	Oak Grove............	1,000 00	....	1,000 00
J. G. Beard...............	Avalon	1,050 00	....	1,050 00
M. L. Anderson...........	Rosendale	55 00	....	55 00
		$16,654 00	$15 00	$16,669 00

Churches not reported, 23.

PRESBYTERY OF POTOSI.

Ministers.	Churches.	Home Objects.	General Objects.	Total.
T. D. Davis...............	Ironton...............	$147 50	$6 00	$153 50
J. Spencer................	Irondale, First........	67 00	5 00	72 00
....	Marble Hill...........	65 00	....	65 00
P. H. Powelson...........	Lake Spring..........	400 00	....	400 00
....	White Water..........	50 00	....	50 00
William Ellers	Mine La Motte	2,300 00	....	2,300 00
		$3,029 50	$11 00	$3,040 50

Churches not reported, 9.

PRESBYTERY OF ST. LOUIS.

Ministers.	Churches.	Home Objects.	General Objects.	Total.
Charles A. Dickey.........	St. Louis, First	$10,300 00	....	$10,300 00
Samuel J. Niccolls, D.D...	St. Louis, Second	26,000 00	$17,010 00	43,010 00
S. M. Morton.............	St. Louis, North......	2,800 00	400 00	3,200 00
Thomas Marshall..........	St. Louis, High St....	5,000 00	....	5,000 00
A. Vander Lippe..........	St. Louis, German.....	1,600 00	....	1,600 00
E. A. Elfeld	Emanuel...............	190 30	....	190 30
William Porteus...........	Calvary (St. Louis)....	2,100 00	....	2,100 00
John R. Warner...........	Kirkwood..............	1,260 00	5 00	1,265 00
F. J. Reichert	Nazareth, German.....	60 00	....	60 00
James M. Smith	St. Charles, First......	9,000 00	13,000 00	22,000 00
....	Bethel..................	....	5 00	5 00
Jacob Schwartz...........	Bethlehem.............	214 85	10 00	224 85
....	Welsh, First..........	162 60	....	162 60
Robert A. Condit..........	Carondelet............	....	2,170 00	2,170 00
J. F. Fenton.............	Cove	....	5 00	5 00
Henry B. Holmes.........	Rock Hill.............	4,003 00	....	4,003 00
R. Kessler................	Webster Groves.......	2,700 00	120 00	2,820 00
Andrew Luce.............	Rolla..................	....	106 00	106 00
John H. Dillingham.......	Fairmount............	1,800 00	....	1,800 00
....	Winsor Harbor Chapel.	1,100 00	....	1,100 00
....	Ferguson..............	2,200 00	....	2,200 00
J. F. Fenton.............	Union	73 30	....	73 30
		$70,564 05	$32,831 00	$103,395 05

Churches not reported, 18.

SYNOD OF NEW JERSEY.

PRESBYTERY OF ELIZABETH.

Ministers.	Churches.	Home Objects.	General Objects.	Total.
Orlando L. Kirtland	Springfield	....	$69 00	$69 00
Robert Street	Connecticut Farms	$377 30	117 00	494 30
Samuel S. Sheddan, D.D.	Rahway, First	6,000 00	....	6,000 00
John A. Liggett	Rahway, Second	....	3,500 00	3,500 00
J. T. English	Liberty Corner	740 00	....	740 00
E. H. Reinhart	Elizabethport	....	25 00	25 00
E. B. Edgar	Westfield	....	560 00	560 00
Geo. C. Lucas	Woodbridge	2,500 00	....	2,500 00
J. B. Patterson	Elizabeth, Second	16,000 00	525 00	16,525 00
E. Kempshall, D.D.	Elizabeth, First	8,400 00	200 00	8,600 00
Wm. C. Roberts, D.D.	Elizabeth, Westminster	21,050 00	6,200 00	27,250 00
G. S. Plumley	Metuchen	1,500 00	216 50	1,716 50
J. G. Williamson	Bethlehem	14,500 00	....	14,500 00
K. P. Ketcham	Plainfield, First	....	70 00	70 00
John C. Bliss	Plainfield, Second	16,000 00	525 40	16,525 40
John Ewing	Clinton	2,150 00	100 00	2,250 00
Thomas Carter	Pluckamin	....	500 00	500 00
Aaron Pack	Perth Amboy	....	60 00	60 00
C. A. Briggs	Roselle	2,500 00	560 00	3,060 00
T. De Hart Bruen	Summit Central	7,350 00	....	7,350 00
		$99,067 30	$13,227 90	$112,295 20

Churches not reported, 9.

—o—

PRESBYTERY OF JERSEY CITY.

Ministers.	Churches.	Home Objects.	General Objects.	Total.
Henry M. Booth	Englewood	....	$11,638 00	$11,638 00
George Brayton	Norwood	$417 80	....	417 80
Samuel W. Duffield	Claremont	1,700 00	....	1,700 00
E. P. Gardner	Hoboken	725 00	....	725 00
J. C. Egbert	Hoboken, West	2,200 00	....	2,200 00
Edward W. French	Bergen, First	6,613 01	....	6,613 01
C. K. Imbrie, D.D.	Jersey City, First	....	1,950 00	1,950 00
I. B. Hopwood	Paterson, Second	816 00	....	816 00
P. F. Leavens	Passaic	3,706 00	....	3,706 00
W. H. Megie	Newfoundland	818 00	....	818 00
G. L. Smith	Rutherford Park	1,935 00	....	1,935 00
James Harkness	Jersey City, Third	1,201 00	....	1,201 00
		$20,131 81	$13,588 00	$33,719 81

Churches not reported, 8.

PRESBYTERY OF MONMOUTH.

Ministers.	Churches.	Home Objects.	General Objects.	Total.
Isaac Tyler	Holmanville	$146 00	$33 00	$179 00
C. F. Worrell, D.D.	Squam Village	378 00	....	378 00
James Petrie	Manchester	....	151 00	151 00
Samuel Miller, D.D.	Mount Holly	905 33	....	905 33
T. Wilson	Shrewsbury	800 00	....	800 00
A. H. Dashiell, Jr.	Bricksburg	450 00	100 00	550 00
J. B. Davis	Hightstown	616 00	267 00	883 00
Joseph G. Symmes	Cranbury, First	....	990 15	990 15
Joseph S. Vandyke	Cranbury, Second	2,250 00	....	2,250 00
A. P. Cobb	Tennent	1,353 00	....	1 253 00
Frank Chandler	Freehold Village	25,000 00	250 00	25,250 00
Joseph W. Hubbard	Dayton	2,200 00	....	2,200 00
John R. Hamilton	Red Bank	350 00	....	350 00
Benj. S. Everitt	Jamesburg	2,500 00	200 00	2,700 00
J. Henry Kaufman	Matawan	1,300 00	200 00	1,500 00
....	Bordentown	....	15 00	15 00
Edward B. Hodge	Burlington	....	400 00	400 00
S. R. Anderson	Tuckerton	1,155 00	....	1,155 00
H. R. Hall	Columbus	102 00	....	102 00
John Brash	South Amboy	2,607 00	....	2,607 00
M. L. Hofford	Fairview	155 00	....	155 00
....	Fairfield	467 00	....	467 00
		$42,734 33	$2,606 15	$45,340 48

Churches not reported, 11.

———o———

PRESBYTERY OF NEWARK.

Ministers.	Churches.	Home Objects.	General Objects.	Total.
J. F. Stearns, D.D.	Newark, First	$10,000 00	$2,500 00	$12,500 00
J. P. Wilson, D.D.	Newark, South Park	9,721 35	1,501 86	11,223 21
J. H. McIlvaine, D.D.	Newark, High Street	10,000 00	....	10,000 00
W. T. Findley, D.D.	Newark, Central	3,100 00	900 00	4,000 00
J. Few Smith, D.D.	Newark, Second	9,400 00	1,500 00	10,900 00
E. R. Craven, D.D.	Newark, Third	314 00	7,092 00	7,406 00
H. N. Brinsmade, D.D.	Newark, Wickliffe	100 00	1,140 00	1,240 00
M. F. Hollister	Newark, Sixth	6,050 00	....	6.050 00
J. U. Guenther	Newark, German First	....	115 00	115 00
Geo. C. Seibert, D.D.	Newark, German Th'd	....	200 00	200 00
Charles T. Haley	Roseville	11,886 00	3,500 00	15,386 00
Charles T. Berry	Caldwell	....	1,752 00	1.752 00
Charles E. Knox	Bloomfield	2,653 43	4,897 70	7.551 13
Duncan Kennedy, D.D.	Westminster, Bloomfl'd	5,500 00	256 00	5,756 00
J. Romeyn Berry, D.D.	Mont Clair	....	6,200 00	6,200 00
George C. Pollock	Lyon's Farms	2,054 00	....	2,054 00
Walter Condict	Newark, Calvary	2,161 20	26 00	2,187 20
Clarence Eddy	Woodside	21 90	28 10	50 00
John M. Ennslin	Bloomfield, German	250 00	100 00	350 00
		$73,211 88	$31,708 66	$104,920 54

Churches not reported, 3.

PRESBYTERY OF MORRIS AND ORANGE.

Ministers.	Churches.	Home Objects.	General Objects.	Total.
J. M. Ogden, D.D.	Chatham	$3,000 00	....	$3,000 00
O. H. P. Deyo.	Dover	24,000 00	$50 00	24,050 00
D. E. Megie	Boonton	1,824 64	61 00	1,885 64
Charles A. Smith, D.D.	East Orange	2,850 00	500 00	3,350 00
Robert Aikman	Madison	....	2,000 00	2,000 00
E. W. Stoddard	Succasunna	405 00	25 00	430 00
O. H. P. Deyo	Rockaway	4,500 00	54 00	4,554 00
Nathaniel Conklin	New Vernon	700 00	314 00	1,014 00
Eldridge Mix	Orange, First	7,082 25	90 00	7,172 25
Henry F. Hickok	Orange, Second	11,689 54	400 00	12,089 54
Alfred Yeomans	Orange, Central	40,000 00	10,000 00	50,000 00
J. Allen Maxwell	Orange, South	3,600 00	240 00	3,840 00
J. Alstyne Blauvelt	German Valley	9,000 00	....	9,000 00
M. Ayers Depue	Pleasant Grove	2,000 00	1,800 00	3,800 00
John A. French	Morristown, First	3,500 00	3,000 00	6,500 00
Albert Erdman	Morristown, South St.	1,366 87	4,761 03	6,127 90
J. A. Ferguson	Hanover, First	1,200 00	27 00	1,227 00
J. W. Cochran	Mendham, First	....	1,400 00	1,400 00
D. K. Freeman	Mendham, Second	970 00	100 00	1,070 00
Daniel W. Fox	Flanders	2,000 00	....	2,000 00
R. S. Feagles	Mt. Olive	3,000 00	....	3,000 00
D. McGee Bardwell	Whippany	....	100 00	100 00
James F. Brewster	Chester	815 00	50 00	865 00
R. S. Rosenthal	Orange, German	3,200 00	....	3,200 00
John R. Willox	Fairmount	1,250 00	....	1,250 00
		$127,953 30	$24,972 03	$152,925 33

Churches not reported, 5.

—o—

PRESBYTERY OF NEW BRUNSWICK.

Ministers.	Churches.	Home Objects.	General Objects.	Total.
J. M. MacDonald, D.D.	Princeton, First	$1,750 00	$328 00	$2,078 00
S. L. Finney	Princeton, Second	1,000 00	10,035 00	11,035 00
John Hall, D.D	Trenton, First	1,450 00	2,020 00	3,470 00
James B. Kennedy	Trenton, Second	450 00	....	450 00
S. M. Studdiford	Trenton, Third	229 38	2,072 00	2,301 38
Richard H. Richardson, D.D	Trenton, Fourth	2,100 00	191 73	2,291 73
A. D. L. Jewitt	New Brunswick, First.	400 00	205 00	605 00
Abraham Gosman, D.D	Lawrenceville	....	160 00	160 00
D. L. Foster	Pennington	494 00	165 50	659 50
A. L. Armstrong	Dutch Neck	550 00	....	550 00
P. A. Studdiford	Lambertville	1,639 48	510 53	2,150 01
Nathaniel L. Upham	Aimwell, First	408 50	25 00	513 50
J. B. Adams	Aimwell, Second	....	33 00	33 00
J. D. Hewitt	Kirkpatrick Memorial.	....	....	....
Geo. S. Mott	Flemington	8,267 00	675 00	8,942 00
William Swan	Stockton	3,800 00	....	3,800 00
J. D. Randolph	Frenchtown	2,000 00	....	2,000 00
J. T. Osler	Kingwood	765 00	....	765 00
John Burrows	Milford	2,306 00	25 00	2,331 00
John Burrows	Holland	835 50	....	835 50
J. V. W. Schenck	Hamilton Square	1,888 89	....	1,888 89
		$30,413 75	$16,445 76	$46,859 51

Churches not reported, 9.

PRESBYTERY OF NEWTON.

Ministers.	Churches.	Home Objects.	General Objects.	Total.
Joel Campbell	Lafayette	$977 00	$123 00	$1,100 00
Andrew Tully	Wautage, Second	700 00	....	700 00
James McWilliam	Deckertown	3,000 00	....	3,000 00
David Tully	Belvidere, First	435 00	320 00	755 00
J. M. Anderson	Belvidere, Second	7,500 00	10 00	7,510 00
E. Clarke Cline	Oxford, Second	9,100 17	296 00	9,396 17
Thomas McCauly	Hackettstown	6,500 00	5,000 00	11,500 00
T. L. Byington	Newton	20,000 00	....	20,000 00
Alanson A. Haines	Hardiston	2,500 00	....	2,500 00
A. H. Holloway	Danville	550 00	16 43	566 43
J. B. Kugler	Musconetcong Valley	50 00	5 00	55 00
P. B. Bonney	Branchville	1,299 60	....	1,299 60
W. C. Stitt	Yellow Frame	4,000 00	....	4,000 00
A. M. Jelly	Mansfield, First	3,000 00	....	3,000 00
Thomas A. Sauson	Blairstown	....	10,206 00	10,206 00
H. B. Townsend	Phillipsburg	946 00	....	946 00
P. H. Brooks	Knowlton	1,751 00	15 00	1,766 00
Wm. Laurie	Stewartsville	....	445 00	445 00
David Conway	Andover	800 00	....	800 00
John J. Crane	Stanhope	....	28 00	28 00
		$63,108 77	$16,46 443	$79,573 20

Churches not reported, 14.

—o—

PRESBYTERY OF WEST JERSEY.

Ministers.	Churches.	Home Objects.	General Objects.	Total.
....	Greenwich	$2,600 00	....	$2,600 00
F. D. Harris	Woodbury	1,000 00	....	1,000 00
....	Pittsgrove	1,625 00	$25 00	1,650 00
F. R. Brace	Blackwoodtown	....	896 00	896 00
C. R. Gregory, D.D.	Bridgeton, First	....	3,639 00	3,639 00
Heber H. Beadle	Bridgeton, Second	539 50	....	539 50
William Bannard, D.D.	Salem	5,000 00	....	5,000 00
J. H. Clark	Cedarville, First	....	45 00	45 00
L. H. Parsons	Cedarville, Second	1,000 00	....	1,000 00
V. D. Reed, D.D.	Camden, First	30,369 00	....	30,369 00
L. C. Baker	Camden, Second	6,750 00	....	6,750 00
Henry Reeves	Gloucester City	1,202 00	....	1,202 00
Robert J. Burtt	Woodstown	207 00	....	207 00
S. W. Pratt	Hammonton	30 00	....	30 00
J. O. Wells	Vineland	....	15 00	15 00
George Warrington	Glassborough	136 00	....	136 00
		$50,458 50	$4,620 00	$55,078 50

Churches not reported, 21.

SYNOD OF NEW YORK.

PRESBYTERY OF BOSTON.

Ministers.	Churches.	Home Objects.	General Objects.	Total.
Ira C. Tyson	Bedford	$1,117 00		$1,117 00
Jas. B. Dunn	Boston, First	5,420 08	$600 00	6,020 08
	Boston, Third		750 00	750 00
Jas. Richards, D.D.	East Boston, First	5,365 60		5,365 40
Wm. House	Londonderry	675 30	153 00	628 30
Joseph Lanman	Windham		233 50	233 50
		$12,377 98	$1,736 50	$14,114 48

Churches not reported, 5.

——o——

PRESBYTERY OF HUDSON.

Ministers.	Churches.	Home Objects.	General Objects.	Total.
D. O. Timlow	Amity	$1,655 00		$1,655 00
W. A. Westcott	Bloomingburg		$26 25	26 25
F. A. Crane	Callicoon	90 00		90 00
C. D. Rosenthal	Clarkstown		25 25	25 25
Thos. Nichols	Chester	1,450 00	350 00	1,800 00
Theron Brittain	Cochecton	302 00		302 00
O. M. Johnson	Denton	505 00	55 00	560 00
George Pierson	Florida		503 00	503 00
J. M. Dickson	Goodwill	6,500		6,500 00
Thos. J. Evans	Greenbush		225 00	225 00
S. C. Hepburn	Hamptonburg	800 00		800 00
A. S. Freeman	Haverstraw, Central		601 30	601 30
John Turner	Hopewell		12 00	12 00
H. Rahn	Jeffersonville, German		25 00	25 00
J. N. Husted	Liberty	1,800 00		1,800 00
A. Seward, D.D	Middletown, First		146 00	146 00
Chas. Beattie	Middletown, Second	120 00	7 00	127 00
D. N. Freeland	Monroe	1,390 00		1,390 00
Luther Littell	Mt. Hope	450 00	50 00	500 00
Richard Bentley	Montgomery	1,200 00		1,200 00
T. M. Dawson	Monticello	4,952 00		4,952 00
Francis L. Patton	Nyack	3,000 00		3,000 00
A. H. Hand, D.D	Palisades	900 00		900 00
A. P. Botsford	Port Jervis			
G. B. Bell	Ramapo		105 00	105 00
D. Beattie	Scotchtown	25 00		25 00
J. J. McMahan	Stony Point	200 00		200 00
Geo. E. Northrup	Waldberg	800 00		800 00
	Washingtonville	150 00	150 00	300 00
D. C. Niven	West Town	44 00		44 00
E. B. Wells	White Lake	100 00		100 00
Thomas Mack	Hemstead	150 00		150 00
		$26,583 00	$2,280 80	$28,863 80

Churches not reported, 11.

PRESBYTERY OF NEW YORK.

Ministers.	Churches.	Home Objects.	General Objects.	Total.
W. W. Newell, D.D.	Allen St.	....	$781 38	$781 38
Gardiner Spring, D.D.; J. O. Murray, D.D.	Brick	$650 00	72,121 61	72,771 61
David Mitchell	Canal Street	1,200 00	....	1,200 00
J. D. Wilson	Central	2,200 00	....	2,200 00
Wm. Adams, D.D.	Madison Square	44,000 00	128,200 00	172,200 00
C. H. Payson	Mad. Sq. Ch. Miss. Ch.	10,000 00	....	10,000 00
....	Manhattanville	500 00	....	500 00
Geo. L. Prentiss, D.D.	Ch. of the Covenant	15,433 00	155,100 00	170,533 00
....	Sea and Land	707 55	....	707 55
H. B. Chapin, D.D.	84th Street	800 00	....	800 00
C. S. Robinson, D.D.	11th St. Ch., or "Mem'l"	75,000 00	....	75,000 00
John Hall, D.D.	5th Ave. and 19th St.	39,088 00	62,357 00	101,445 00
....	42d Street	700 00	100 00	800 00
E. W. Hitchcock	14th Street	....	6,178 37	6,178 37
John Thomson, D.D.	Fourth (34th Street.)	10,696 00	1,000 00	11,696 00
Howard Crosby, D.D.	Fourth Avenue	7,275 00	5,525 00	12,800 00
B. Krusi	German	25 00	....	25 00
T. A. Leggett	Harlem	5,525 75	....	5,525 75
Thos. Street	North	20,000 00	....	20,000 00
S. D. Alexander, D.D.	Phillips	300 00	280 00	580 00
N. W. Conklin	Rutgers	3,500 00	1,600 00	5,100 00
Wm. Aikman, D.D.	Spring Street	....	800 00	800 00
S. D. Burchard, D.D.	13th Street	....	1,500 00	1,500 00
W. W. Page	Thomp'n & Houston St	1,080 00	....	1,080 00
H. D. Northrop	West 23d Street	2,200 00	300 00	2,500 00
R. R. Booth, D.D.	University Place	16,851 80	61,485 00	78,336 80
Chas. A. Stoddard	Washington Heights	1,708 00	1,000 00	2,708 00
Thomas S. Hastings, D.D.	West	24,720 25	....	24,720 25
G. S. Chambers	Murray Hill (40th St)	1,558 23	200 00	1,758 23
		$285,718 58	$498,618 45	$784,246 94

Churches not reported, 13.

——o——

PRESBYTERY OF NORTH RIVER.

Ministers.	Churches.	Home Objects.	General Objects.	Total.
G. P. Noble	Malden	$150 00	....	$150 00
W. N. Page	Armenia	7,000 00	$100 00	7,100 00
Wm. A. Halliday	Bethlehem	787 00	43 00	830 00
J. Silliman	Canterbury	3,000 00	26 00	3,026 00
John W. Teal	Cornwall	2,111 00	....	2,111 00
O. H. Hazard	Freedom Plains	400 00	....	400 00
E. P. Roe	Highlands	1,469 07	....	1,469 07
H. B. Holmes	Kingston	148 75	5 00	153 75
R. H Wallace	Little Britain	1,250 00	250 00	1,500 00
Charles W. Cooper	Marlborough	605 00	25 00	630 00
F. R. Masters, D.D.	Matteawan	2,400 00	25 00	2,425 00
Joseph H. Myers, D.D.	Milton	500 00	....	500 00

Continued on next page.

PRESBYTERY OF NORTH RIVER.—CONTINUED.

Ministers.	Churches.	Home Objects.	General Objects.	Total.
Wm. T. Sprole, D.D.	Newburgh, First	....	$500 00	$500 00
Wendell Prime	Newburgh, Union	$20,000 00	....	20,000 00
W. N. Sayre	Pine Plains	1,000 00	....	1,000 00
H. J. Acker	Pleasant Valley	642 00	....	642 00
F. B. Wheeler, D.D.	Poughkeepsie, First	4,258 05	535 30	4,793 35
E. D. Ledyard	Rondout	....	575 00	575 00
S. N. Hutchinson	Salt Point, Westminster	1,200 00	91 00	1,291 00
Harvey Smith	South Armenia	1,200 00	....	1,200 00
A. H. Seeley	Smithfield	300 00	....	300 00
O. A. Kingsbury	Wappinger's Falls	53 00	....	53 00
		$48,462 87	$2,175 30	$50,648 17

Churches not reported, 10.

———o———

PRESBYTERY OF WESTCHESTER.

Ministers.	Churches.	Home Objects.	General Objects.	Total.
P. B. Heroy	Bedford	....	$250 00	$250 00
Horace G. Hinsdale	Bridgeport, First	....	918 51	918 51
Wm. J. Thompson	Croton Falls	$65 00	225 00	290 00
Jas. W. Coleman	Darien	200 00	....	200 00
T. M. Niven, Jr.	Dobb's Ferry	900 00	....	900 00
R. W. Dickinson	Ft. Washington	650 00	500 00	1,150 00
D. D. Sahler	Gilead	200 00	....	200 00
T. Aspinwall Hodge	Hartford, First	5,500 00	....	5,500 00
R. A. Sawyer	Irvington	6,000 00	4,000 00	10,000 00
John Hancock	Mt. Kisco	1,200 00	100 00	1,300 00
E. R. Burkhalter	New Rochelle	400 00	1,000 00	1,400 00
Chas. H. Holloway	North Salem	100 00	10 00	110 00
James Baird, D.D.	Paterson	183 00	....	183 00
Jno. N. Freeman	Peekskill, First	16,500 00	....	16,500 00
Nelson Millard	Peekskill, Second	12,300 00	....	12,300 00
Ezra F. Munday	Portchester	1,822 25	18 44	1,840 69
Arthur Potts	Morrisania	850 00	....	850 00
Chas. W. Baird	Rye	40,636 25	2,000 00	42,636 25
Wilson Phraner	Sing Sing	3,000 00	500 00	3,500 00
A. R. Macoubrey	Southeast, Centre	226 25	228 50	454 75
D. S. Gregory	South Salem	250 00	414 00	664 00
A. S. Twombly	Stamford, First	2,500 00	467 60	2,967 60
Hen. F. Lee	Thompsonville, First	720 00	....	720 00
Alex. Nesbitt	Fremont	2,950 00	....	2,950 00
George Nixon	West Farms	5,100 00	....	5,100 00
T. Ralston Smith, D.D.	Yonkers, First	6,150 00	450 00	6,600 00
Lewis W. Mudge	Yonkers, Westminster	468 00	....	468 00
Jas. W. Johnston	Yorktown	3,000 00	....	3,000 00
		$111,870 75	$11,082 05	$122,952 80

Churches not reported, 10.

SYNOD OF PACIFIC.

PRESBYTERY OF BENICIA.

Ministers.	Churches.	Home Objects.	General Objects.	Total.
Robt. McCulloch..........	Big Valley............	$9,842 00	....	$9,842 00
R. R. Wells...............	Healdsburgh..........	350 00	....	350 00
C. S. Dewing..............	Mendocino...........	650 00	....	650 00
Richard Wylie	Napa.................	....	$400 00	400 00
T. E. Taylor..............	San Rafael...........	585 00	....	585 00
L. P. Whiting.............	Santa Rosa...........	822 50	....	822 50
....	Two Rocks...........	300 00	....	300 00
N. B. Klink...............	Vallejo...............	650 00	....	650 00
J. S. Todd................	Arcata...............	550 00	....	550 00
Robt. McCulloch..........	Shiloh...............	720 00	....	720 00
		$14,469 50	$400 00	$14,869 50

Churches not reported, 2.

—o—

PRESBYTERY OF OREGON.

Ministers.	Churches.	Home Objects.	General Objects.	Total.
M. A. Williams............	Jackson	$400 50	$50 00	$450 50
R. Robe	Brownsville...........	75 00	....	75 00
....	Corvallis.	....	100 00	100 00
....	Eugene City..........	....	108 75	108 75
J. R. Thompson...........	Olympia..............	661 00	....	661 00
A. L. Lindsley, D.D.......	Portland..............	1,427 00	....	1,427 00
G. W. Sloan...............	Steilicoom	262 00	....	262 00
....	Phenix................	30 00	....	30 00
		$2,855 50	$258 75	$3,114 25

Churches not reported, 5.

PRESBYTERY OF SACRAMENTO.

Ministers.	Churches.	Home Objects.	General Objects.	Total.
A. Fairbairn	Chico	$8,129 00		$8,129 00
John Brown	Elko	2,950 00		2,950 00
Lewis Thompson	Ione Valley	58 00	$25 00	83 00
W. W. McKaig	Marysville	5,000 00		5,000 00
James M. Newell	Placerville	570 00		570 00
F. L. Nash	Sacramento	375 00	550 00	925 00
B. E. S. Ely	Stockton	3,250 00		3,250 00
W. W. Macomber	Virginia City	20 00	150 00	170 00
B. S. Lowe	Rio Visto		10 00	10 00
James Woods	Amador	1,250 00		1,250 00
W. W. Brier	Westminster	925 00		925 00
		$22,527 00	$735 00	$23,262 00

Churches not reported, 11.

—o—

PRESBYTERY OF SAN JOSÉ.

Ministers.	Churches.	Home Objects.	General Objects.	Total.
L. P. Webber	Anaheim	$100 00		$100 00
A. M. Stewart	Gilroy	1,500 00		1,500 00
	San Buena Ventura	215 00		215 00
L. S. McDonald	San Diego	1,344 00		1,344 00
Wm. Alexander	San José	7,200 00		7,200 00
A. H. White, LL.D	San Leandro	550 00		550 00
H. H. Dobbins	Santa Barbara	1,656 00		1,656 00
A. B. Post	Santa Clara	1,527 00		1,527 00
	Tomales	2,000 00		2,000 00
	Tule River		$40 00	40 00
	Visalia	800 00		800 00
	Watsonville	400 00		400 00
	Milpitas	712 00		712 00
	Centerville		132 00	132 00
	Livermore	300 00		300 00
		$18,089 00	$172 00	$18,261 00

Churches not reported, 4.

PRESBYTERY OF SAN FRANCISCO.

Ministers.	Churches.	Home Objects.	General Objects.	Total.
Oliver Hemstreet..........	Brooklyn..............	$505 00	....	$505 00
H. R. Avery	Contra Costa..........	55 00	....	55 00
....	San Francisco, First...	1,483 00	....	1,483 00
....	San Francisco, Calvary	....	$3,500 00	3,500 00
Sylvester Woodbridge, D.D.	San Fran., Howard St..	1,037 91	....	1,037 91
....	San Fran., Howard Ch.	5,180 00	1,812 90	6,992 90
T. M. Cunningham, D.D...	San Francisco, Central	14,000 00	....	14,000 00
Wm. A. Scott, D.D........	San Francisco, St. John	58,600 00	....	58,600 00
A. G. McCarthy...........	San Francisco, Olivet..	500 00	....	500 00
H. W. Loomis.............	San Francisco, Chinese	50 00	25 00	75 00
		$80,537 50	$5,337 90	$85,739 41

Churches not reported, 5.

SYNOD OF PHILADELPHIA.

PRESBYTERY OF CHESTER.

Ministers.	Churches.	Home Objects.	General Objects.	Total.
Robert P. Du Bois.........	New London..........	....	$393 50	$393 55
James W. Dale, D.D.......	Media	$1,000 00	....	1,000 00
Justus T. Umsted	Fogg's Manor.........	1,200 00	....	1,200 00
Wm. E. Moore............	West Chester..........	2,000 00	2,320 00	4,320 00
A. W. Sproull.............	Chester...............	5,185 00	1,643 00	6,828 00
Aug. T. Dobson...........	Chester City...........	700 00	....	700 00
W. F. P. Noble............	Penningtonville.......	125 00	75 00	250 00
Orr Lawson..............	Oxford...............	15,740 00	....	15,740 00
J. W. Porter..............	Phœnixville...........	4,000 00	....	4,000 00
J. J. Pomeroy.............	Upper Octorara.......	5,630 00	....	5,630 00
Wm. A. Ferguson..........	Waynesberg...........	1,540 00	114 60	1,654 60
Edward P. Heberton.......	Great Valley..........	1,580 00	20 00	1,600 00
James Roberts............	Coatesville...........	4,300 00	....	4,300 00
T. J. Aiken...............	Reeseville............	2,700 00	32 00	2,732 00
John Rea.................	Downingtown.........	313 95	....	313 95
A. Nelson Hollifield........	Fairview..............	11,000 00	....	11,000 00
Geo. L. Raymond..........	Darby, Second........	3,052 31	....	3,052 31
C. Forbes.................	U. W. Nottingham....	114 00	....	114 00
L. J. Aiken...............	East Whiteland........	350 00	33 00	383 00
		$60,745 26	$4,631 10	$65,376 36

Churches not reported, 11.

PRESBYTERY OF LEHIGH.

Ministers.	Churches.	Home Objects.	General Objects.	Total.
John White	Summit Hill	$75 00	$25 00	$100 00
E. J. Richards, D.D	Reading, First	6,300 00	270 00	6,570 00
Jacob Belville, D.D	Mauch Chunk	5,875 00	3,010 75	8,885 75
Cornelius Earle	Catasaqua, First	8,500 00	1,056 00	9,556 00
W. Fulton	Catasaqua, Second	1,617 00	25 00	1,642 00
Andrew M. Lowry	Port Carbon	1,000 00	....	1,000 00
D. Stuart Banks	Brainerd, Easton	....	861 00	861 00
David M. James	Allen Township	9,200 00	....	9,200 00
Robt. B. Foresman	L. Mt. Bethel	41 00	....	41 00
W. H. Dinsmore	Stroudsburg	2,626 00	....	2,626 00
D. Deruelle	Weatherly	301 05	16 00	317 05
A. W. Woods	Mahanoy City	2,720 00	118 19	2,838 19
F. E. Miller	Easton, First	1,245 00	1,000 00	2,245 00
B. C. Meeker	Tamaqua	1,590 00	....	1,590 00
Jas. A. Little	Hokendaqua	7,500 00	....	7,500 00
S. W. Knipe	Mountain	500 00	....	500 00
John MacNaughton	Slatington	850 00	....	850 00
Robt. B. Foresman	Bangor	4 00	....	4 00
Geo. H. Hammer	Upper Lehigh	3,000 00	....	3,000 00
J. C. Clyde	Shenandoah	....	10 00	10 00
Richd. Walker	Lockridge	6,000 00	....	6,000 00
....	Hazleton	....	743 25	743 25
		$58,944 05	$7,135 19	$66,079 24

Churches not reported, 15.

—o—

PRESBYTERY OF LACKAWANNA.

Ministers.	Churches.	Home Objects.	General Objects.	Total.
Edward Allen	Gibson	$1,400 00	....	$1,400 00
Geo. Spaulding	Brooklyn	5,000 00	....	5,000 00
....	Barclay	754 50	....	754 50
T. Thomas	Rushville	25 00	5 00	30 00
D. Cook	Wyalusing, First	400 00	....	400 00
H. Armstrong	Munroeton	115 00	....	115 00
David Craft	Wyalusing, Second	4,550 00	....	4,550 00
J. Cory	Abington	1,460 00	....	1,460 00
H. Van Houten	Hawley	....	22 25	22 25
Clark Salmon	Meshoppen	261 00	....	261 00
S. C. Logan, D.D	Scranton, First	2,407 50	28,290 50	30,698 00
N. G. Parke	Pittston	2,384 29	....	2,384 29
E. O. Ward	Bethany	128 00	....	128 00
S. P. Gates	Canton	143 00	100 00	243 00
Stephen A. Califf	Wells and Columbia	512 25	....	512 25
....	Athens	100 00	....	100 00
Joel Jewell	Columbia Cross Roads	....	5 00	5 00
J. Best	Waymart	....	25 00	25 00
J. Best	Prompton	107 00	....	107 00
G. C. Judson	Franklin	152 25	180 00	332 25
J. S. Stewart	Towanda	5,238 00	2,312 00	7,550 00
W. P. Gibson	Kingston	6,320 00	....	6,320 00

Continued on next page.

PRESBYTERY OF LACKAWANNA.—CONTINUED.

Ministers.	Churches.	Home Objects.	General Objects.	Total.
J. G. Miller	Montrose	$800 00	$125 00	$925 00
A. B. King	Wyoming	50 00	1,314 00	1,364 00
William J. Day	Coalville	1,400 00	....	1,400 00
Jas. W. Raynor	Mt. Pleasant	361 00	....	361 00
....	Uniondale	140 00	....	140 00
Chas. S. Dunning, D.D.	Honesdale	7,500 00	....	7,500 00
F. B. Hodge	Willkesbarre	16,023 00	717 00	16,740 00
A. G. Harned	Newton	724 96	160 00	884 96
J. E. Lang	Archibald, German	1,149 00	....	1,149 00
J. B. Fisher	Providence	502 00	....	502 00
B. S. Foster	Dunmore	715 00	....	715 00
A. D. Barber	New Milford	650 00	....	650 00
S. H. Moon	Susquehanna	522 50	35 00	557 50
E. D. Bryan	Carbondale	2,500 00	....	2,500 00
W. P. White	Plymouth	2,300 00	....	2,300 00
....	Orwell	220 05	....	220 05
		$67,015 30	$33,290 75	$100,306 05

Churches not reported, 29.

——o——

PRESBYTERY OF PHILADELPHIA, NORTH.

Ministers.	Churches.	Home Objects.	General Objects.	Total.
J. Foster Halsey, D.D.	Norristown, First	$687 56	$290 00	$977 56
Jas. H. Symmes	Conshohocken	3,378 59	....	3,378 59
S. M. Andrews, D.D.	Doylest'n & Deep Run.	25,000 00	64 35	25,064 35
H. S. Rodenbough	Norrist'n & Providence	2,400 00	....	2,400 00
H. S. Rodenbough	Port Kennedy	....	5 00	5 00
R. Owen, D.D.	Chestnut Hill	....	4,000 00	4,000 00
Geo. C. Bush	Newtown	242 00	295 37	537 37
Addison V. C. Schenk	Kenderton	2,000 00	....	2,000 00
Thos. Murphy	Frankford	900 00	500 00	1,400 00
G. H. Nimmo	Neshaminy (Warm'st'r)	565 00	....	575 00
Joseph Beggs	Falls of Schuylkill	2,500 00	....	2,500 00
Samuel T. Lowrie	Abington	2,090 86	5 00	2,095 86
H. T. Ford	Norristown Central	1,000 00	....	1,000 00
John C. Thompson	Pottstown	2,000 00	....	2,000 00
W. A. Jenks	Bridesberg	5,000 00	....	5,000 00
C. Collins	Jeffersonville	100 00	....	100 00
A. McCullagh	Germantown, Second	2,677 00	300 00	2,977 00
Edw'd P. Cowan	Germant'n, Market Sq.	1,635 00	2,530 00	4,165 00
Jacob Weidman	Bristol	375 00	125 00	500 00
D. K. Turner	Neshaminy (Warwick).	300 00	....	300 00
T. C. Anderson	Huntingdon Valley	130 00	....	130 00
Jacob B. Krewson	Forestville	300 00	....	300 00
J. F. Dripps	Germantown, First	23,300 00	1,700 00	25,000 00
F. R. S. Hunsicker	Plumstedville	350 00	5 50	355 50
		$76,941 01	$9,820 22	$86,761 23

Churches not reported, 12.

PRESBYTERY OF PHILADELPHIA, CENTRAL.

Ministers.	Churches.	Home Objects.	General Objects.	Total.
W. W. Taylor............	Philadelphia, Olivet...	....	$295 50	$295 50
Thos. J. Shepherd, D.D....	Philad'a, N. Lib., First	$1,407 28	1,740 20	3,147 48
Geo. F. Wiswell, D.D.....	Philad'a, Green Hill...	18,000 00	....	18,000 00
Wm. O. Johnstone........	Philad'a, Kensington..	5,800 00	....	5,800 00
W. T. Eva............	Philad'a, Bethesda....	17,193 00	....	17,193 00
A. A. Willits, D.D.........	Philad'a, West Arch St.	60,000 00	....	60,000 00
Jas. Y. Mitchell	Philad'a, N. Lib., Cent'l	10,293 75	....	10,293 75
Alex. Reed, D.D...........	Philadelphia, Central..	8,937 55	1,066 00	10,003 55
D. A. Cunningham........	Philad'a, Spring Garden	....	20 00	20 00
Benj. L. Agnew...........	Philadelphia, North...	6,816 00	20 00	6,836 00
S. A. Mutchmore, D.D.....	Philad'a, Cohocksink..	10,000 00	....	10,000 00
H. A. Smith	Philad'a, Mantua, First	3,884 00	....	3,884 00
Frank L. Robbins..........	Philadelphia, Oxford..	30,500 00	....	30,500 00
J. Addison Henry.........	Phila., Princeton......	4,153 00	40 00	4,193 00
J. H. Beale...............	Phil., Kensington, First	6,041 00	....	6,041 00
Matthew Newkirk.........	Philad'a, N. 10th St...	2,425 00	75 00	2,500 00
J. L. Withrow............	Philadelphia, Arch St..	19,000 00	610 00	19,610 00
Geo. F. Cain..............	Philad'a, Alexander...	32,000 00	....	32,000 00
....	Philadelphia, Western.	....	2,085 00	2,085 00
R. D. Harper, D.D........	Philad'a, N. Broad St..	15,000 00	3,200 00	18,200 00
		$251,450 58	$9,151 70	$260,602 28

Churches not reported, 8.

——o——

PRESBYTERY OF WESTMINSTER.

Ministers.	Churches.	Home Objects.	General Objects.	Total.
Lindley C. Rutter.........	Chestnut Level........	$125 00	....	$125.000
P. J. Timlow............	Leacock	2,940 00	$300 00	3,240 00
T. M. Crawford...........	Slateville.............	150 00	10 00	160 00
J. M. Rittenhouse.........	Middle Octoraru.......	1,000 00	....	1,000 00
Calvin W. Stewart........	Union	152 50	....	152 50
Henry E. Niles............	York.................	33,000 00	1,000 00	34,000 00
J. Y. Cowhick	Hopewell.............	6,000 00	....	6,000 00
J. Y. Cowhick	Centre...............	200 00	....	200 00
J. Y. Cowhick	Stewartstown	250 00	....	250 00
Joseph D. Smith..........	Slate Ridge...........	15 00	26 00	41 00
S. McNair...............	Little Britain.........	5,000 00	....	5,000 00
Robert Gamble............	Chanceford	300 00	....	300 00
Geo. Robinson............	Lancaster............	2,000 00	....	2,000 00
B. H. Witherow...........	Columbia.............	10,474 00	....	10,474 00
....	Coleraine, Free	....	....	....
S. Morton Pierce..........	Wrightsville	229 79	....	229 79
Alex. F. Morrison.........	New Harmony........	400 00	....	400 00
Sam'l B. Webster..........	Bellevue.............	1,610 00	....	1,610 00
....	Mount Joy...........	30 00	....	30 00
R. P. Shaw..............	Cedar Grove.........	....	20 00	20 00
R. K. M. Baynum.........	Strasburg............	....	25 00	25 00
A. W. Hubbard...........	Dillsbury............	....	23 00	23 00
		$63,876 29	$1,404 00	$65,280 29

Churches not reported, 6.

PRESBYTERY OF PHILADELPHIA.

Ministers.	Churches.	Home Objects.	General Objects.	Total.
Robert Adair..............	Philadelphia, Tabor...	$1,247 00	....	$1,247 00
David Malin, D.D.........	Philadelphia, Fifteenth	3,500 00	....	3,500 00
William Blackwood, D.D...	Philadelphia, Ninth...	2,500 00	....	2,500 00
Daniel March, D.D........	Philad'a, Clinton St...	2,000 00	$210 00	2,210 00
W. P. Breed, D.D.........	Philad'a, West Spruce.	2,967 60	9,467 50	12,435 10
R. H. Allen, D.D..........	Philadelphia, Third...	2,354 85	315 00	2,669 85
Z. M. Humphrey, D.D.....	Philadelphia, Calvary..	6,500 00	53,532 00	60,032 00
W. M. Rice, D.D..........	Philadelphia, Fourth..	800 00	....	800 00
Herrick Johnson, D.D.....	Philadelphia, First....	1,500 00	14,028 90	15,528 90
R. M. Patterson...........	Philadelphia, South....	1,790 00	....	1,790 00
Henry C. McCook..........	Philadelphia, Seventh.	4,421 50	725 00	5,146 50
S. W. Dana...............	Philad'a, Walnut St....	12,500 00	565 00	13,065 00
J. Henry Sharpe..........	Philad'a, Wharton St..	3,050 00	....	3,050 00
James M. Crowell, D.D.....	Philadelphia, Woodland	24,627 00	300 00	24,927 00
		$69,757 95	$79,143 40	$148,901 35

Churches not reported, 14.

SYNOD OF PITTSBURGH.

PRESBYTERY OF BLAIRSVILLE.

Ministers.	Churches.	Home Objects.	General Objects.	Total.
W. J. Bollman............	Congruity.............	$2,575 00	$106 00	$2,681 00
Geo. Hill, D.D...........	Blairsville............	....	930 00	930 00
D. Harbison..............	New Salem,............	....	628 10	628 10
Ross Stevenson...........	Ligonier.............	155 00	25 00	180 00
Ross Stevenson...........	Pleasant Grove........	157 00	....	157 00
Robert Carothers..........	Cross Roads...........	....	333 60	333 60
G. W. Shaiffer...........	Armagh...............	460 00	15 00	475 00
G. W. Shaiffer...........	Centreville...........	90 00	15 00	105 00
J. A. Marshall............	Beulah...............	1,650 00	....	1,650 00
Wm. A. Fleming..........	Johnstown............	500 00	120 00	620 00
G. M. Spargrove..........	Murraysville..........	8,403 00	46 35	8,449 25
T. R. Ewing..............	New Alexandria.......	....	613 00	613 00
J. D. Moorhead...........	Plum Creek...........	....	140 00	140 00
B. M. Kerr...............	Ebensburgh...........	300 00	60 00	360 00
W. F. Hamilton...........	Salem................	92 00	106 00	198 00
W. F. Hamilton...........	Livermore............	45 00	231 00	276 00
D. W. Townsend..........	Unity................	250 00	250 00	500 00
S. M. Davis..............	Latrobe..............	....	400 00	400 00
Henry Bain...............	Poke Run.............	1,650 00	....	1,650 00
....	Harrison City........	....	48 00	48 00
D. G. Robinson...........	Black Lick...........	....	76 00	76 00
J. P. Kennedy............	Parnassus............	....	40 00	40 00
		$16,327 00	$4,182 95	$20,509 95

Churches not reported, 4.

PRESBYTERY OF PITTSBURGH.

Ministers.	Churches.	Home Objects.	General Objects.	Total.
Wm. Smith, D.D.	Miller's Run	....	$151 00	$151 00
J. C. Jennings, D.D.	Sharon	$2,951 68	....	2,951 68
Ezra S. Harney	Mt. Pisgah	5 00	51 00	56 00
Geo. Marshall, D.D.	Bethel	345 00	266 05	611 05
R. Lea	Lawrenceville	560 00	230 00	790 00
....	Hopewell	1,000 00	....	1,000 00
R. S. Morton	Chartiers	55 00	53 00	108 00
C. G. Bradock	Bethamy	4,133 00	217 00	4,350 00
S. F. Scovel	Pittsburg, First	1,071 00	20,440 00	21,511 00
Wm. D. Howard, D.D.	Pittsburg, Second	3,790 02	3,200 35	6,990 37
F. A. Noble	Pittsburg, Third	....	11,184 00	11,184 00
M. W. Jacobus, D.D.	Pittsburg, Central	....	17,500 00	17,500 00
S. J. Wilson, D.D.	Pittsburg, Sixth	4,984 00	1,000 00	5,984 00
James Kirk	Long Island	53 00	....	53 00
W. W. McKinney	Mingo	5,568 00	....	5,568 00
J. J. Beacom	Montours	200 00	100 00	300 00
J. J. Beacom	Forest Grove	900 00	....	900 00
Samuel S. Shriver	Lebanon	8,000 00	6,000 00	14,000 00
W. T. Beatty	Shady Side	6,918 00	11,499 00	18,417 00
....	Valley	1,000 00	....	1,000 00
J. S. Stuchell	Hazlewood	5,173 00	....	5,173 00
Wm. F. Brown	Cannonsburg	75 00	148 68	223 68
P. S. Davies	Birmingham	4,423 00	....	4,423 00
S. M. Henderson	Wilkinsburgh	3,800 00	100 00	3,900 00
P. S. Jennings	Mt. Washington	489 00	....	489 00
James S. Hawk	Westminster	3,939 00	....	3,939 00
P. J. Cummings	Mt. Carmel	4,000 00	....	4,000 00
F. R. Wotring	Mansfield	1,200 00	....	1,200 00
Jno. Gillespie	East Liberty	1,163 00	15,224 00	16,387 00
Samuel Fisher	Swissvale	7,600 00	....	7,600 00
Edward P. Crane	Minersville	158 00	20 00	178 00
Wm. O. Campbell	Monongahela City	4,318 29	....	4,318 29
D. T. Carnahan	Bellefield	5,433 00	90 00	5,523 00
		$83,304 99	$87,474 08	$170,779 07

Churches not reported, 9.

———o———

PRESBYTERY OF WEST VIRGINIA.

Ministers.	Churches.	Home Objects.	General Objects.	Total.
James H. Flanagan	Fairmont	$238 00	....	$238 00
Robert A. Blockford	Clarksburg	70 00	$10 00	80 00
W. R. Libbet	Portland	25 00	655 00	680 00
....	Buckhannon	625 00	100 00	725 00
....	Bethel	50 00	....	50 00
W. R. Libbet	Newburg	150 00	....	150 00
Loyal Young, D.D.	French Creek	....	1,049 96	1,049 96
....	Morgantown	....	42 00	42 00
M. Edgar	Kingwood	42 00	....	42 00
Loyal Young, D.D.	Weston	245 00	....	245 00
J. M. Nourse	Hugh's River	1,500 00	....	1,500 00
J. H. Flanagan	Grafton	113 00	....	113 00
		$3,058 00	$1,856 96	$4,914 96

Churches not reported, 10.

PRESBYTERY OF REDSTONE.

Ministers.	Churches.	Home Objects.	General Objects.	Total.
J. Stoneroad	Laurel Hill	$510 00	$341 00	$851 00
John McClintock	Greensboro		96 00	96 00
Wm. Edgar	Somerset	1,000 00	12 00	1,012 00
J. M. Barnett	Connellsville	4,275 00	1,150 00	5,425 00
H. O. Rosborough	Spring Hill	100 00		100 00
N. H. G. Fife	Long Run	3,500 00		3,500 00
L. Y. Graham	Rehoboth	2,626 00		2,626 00
W. W. Ralston	Uniontown	3,050 00		3,050 00
	Little Redstone	2,660 00		2,660 00
John McMillan, D.D	Mt. Pleasant	20,000 00		20,000 00
	Lent	53 00	1,000 00	1,053 00
Thos. S. Parke	Tyrone	550 00	100 00	650 00
John McClintock	New Providence	266 00	234 00	500 00
G. M. Hair	McKeesport	5,515 00	78 00	5,593 00
H. O. Rosborough	George's Creek	210 00	77 00	287 00
J. P. Fulton	Dunlap's Creek	2,000 00	50 00	2,050 00
J. P. Fulton	McClellandtown	600 00		600 00
	Round Hill	2,000 00		2,000 00
E. P. Lewis	Brownsville	1,317 00		1,317 00
Henry Fulton	West Newton	2,850 00		2,850 00
	Pleasant Unity	1,488 00		1,488 00
	Mt. Washington	100 00		100 00
Asahel Bronson, D.D	Jefferson	5 00		5 00
T. S. Parke	Harmony		25 00	25 00
	Mt. Vernon	1,100 00		1,100 00
		$55,775 00	$3,163 00	$88,938 00

Churches not reported, 3.

PRESBYTERY OF WASHINGTON.

Ministers.	Churches.	Home Objects.	General Objects.	Total.
John Stockton, D.D	Cross Creek	$1,178 00	$603 00	$1,781 00
Alex. McCarrell, D.D	Claysville		50 00	50 00
W. H. Lester	West Alexander	1,200 00	400 00	1,600 00
R. T. Price	Mt. Prospect	5,660 00		5,660 00
D. M. Miller	Cross Roads	983 00	255 50	1,238 50
R. B. Farrar	West Union	1,650 00		1,650 00
A. O. Rockwell	Frankfort	5,425 00	575 00	6,000 00
	Waynesburgh		52 50	52 50
D. W. Fisher	Wheeling, First	7,750 00	291 68	8,041 68
Bellville Roberts	Wheeling, Fourth	405 00		405 00
James J. Brownson, D.D	Washington, First	4,926 16	5,326 02	10,252 18
George P. Hays, D.D	Washington, Second		1,858 37	1,858 37
John Eagleson, D.D	Upper Buffalo	10,225 00	247 00	10,472 00
Smith F. Grier	New Cumberland	103 00		103 00
J. T. Fredericks	Burgettstown	481 00	308 87	789 87
L. Grier	Forks of Wheeling		170 00	170 00
Samuel Graham	Unity		101 50	101 50
R. R. Moore	Wellsburg	1,368 00		1,368 00
John B. Graham	Holliday's Cove	782 00	15 00	797 00
		$42,136 16	$10,254 44	$52,390 60

Churches not reported, 17.

SYNOD OF TENNESSEE.

PRESBYTERY OF AUSTIN.

Ministers.	Churches.	Home Objects.	General Objects.	Total.
J. A. Williams	Austin, First	$4,000 00	$40 00	$4,040 00
		$4,000 00	$40 00	$4,040 00

—o—

PRESBYTERY OF KINGSTON.

Ministers.	Churches.	Home Objects.	General Objects.	Total.
....	Rockford	....	$100 00	$100 00
....	New Providence	$438 00	....	438 00
T. J. Lamar	Forest Hill	....	580 00	580 00
T. J. Lamar	Clover Hill	....	600 00	600 00
....	Baker's Creek	125 00	400 00	525 00
....	....	....	....	....
....	Mount Zion	....	20 00	20 00
....	Madisonville	....	10 00	10 00
David M. Wilson	New Bethel	5 00	....	5 00
David M. Wilson	Mars Hill	35 00	....	35 00
E. W. P. Wyott	Bethel	820 00	....	820 00
....	Grassy Cove	650 00	....	650 00
....	Kingston, Second	....	5 00	5 00
		$2,073 00	$1,715 00	$3,788 00

Churches not reported, 17.

PRESBYTERY OF HOLSTON.

Ministers.	Churches.	Home Objects.	General Objects.	Total.
....	Mount Bethel.........	....	....	....
W. B. Rankin.............	Salem	$1,000 00	$5 00	$1,005 00
J. Bell..................	Lebanon............	50 00	....	50 00
S. V. McCorkle	Kingsport.............	....	15 00	15 00
J. G. Mason	Jonesboro.............	....	59 41	59 41
P. D. Cowan.............	Rogersville	93 75	....	93 75
W. S. Doak...............	Timber Ridge.........	214 25	....	214 25
S. V. McCorkle............	New Salem............	630 00	....	630 00
		$1,988 00	$79 41	$2,067 41

Churches not reported, 7.

—o—

PRESBYTERY OF NEW ORLEANS.

Ministers.	Churches.	Home Objects.	General Objects.	Total.
John H. Hollander........	....	....	....	....
Otto Koelle..............	New Orleans, Second..	....	$123 75	$123 75
			$123 75	$123 75

—o—

PRESBYTERY OF UNION.

Ministers.	Churches.	Home Objects.	General Objects.	Total.
W. H. Lyle...............	Westminster..........	....	$72 35	$72 35
W. H. Lyle...............	Mount Horeb.........	....	165 64	165 64
E. N. Sawtell.............	Hopewell	2,017 11	....	2,017 11
P. D. Cowan.............	New Market..........	102 25	84 50	186 75
Isaac A. Martin..........	Caledonia.............	150 00	....	150 00
E. N. Sawtell.	Washington...........	....	235 00	235 00
E. S. Herron..............	Spring Place..........	....	15 00	15 00
N. Bachman..............	Knoxville, Second.....	4,058 34	....	4,058 34
....	New Prospect.........	1,031 00	....	1,031 00
		$7,358 70	$572 49	$7,931 19

Churches not reported, 11.

SYNOD OF TOLEDO.

PRESBYTERY OF BELLEFONTAINE.

Ministers.	Churches.	Home Objects.	General Objects.	Total.
J. P. Lloyd...............	Crestline..............	$625 00	....	$625 00
J. H. Sherrard............	Bucyrus...............	100 00	$403 58	503 58
John B. Blayney..........	Upper Sandusky......	365 00	....	365 00
L. J. Drake...............	West Liberty..........	258 00	....	258 00
A. Telford................	Spring Hills..........	160 70	114 00	274 70
Geo. L. Kalb.............	Bellefontaine,.........	1,400 00	....	1,400 00
J. G. Hall....	Kenton................	1,000 00	....	1,000 00
H. M. Shockley..........	Belle Centre...........	924 00	....	924 00
H. M. Shockley..........	Huntsville.............	183 00	....	183 00
J. C. Meloy........	Buck Creek...........	21 00	180 00	201 00
J. A. P. McGaw..........	Urbana...............	1,482 00	820 00	2,302 00
J. G. Junkin.............	Wyandotte............	....	25 00	25 00
....	Eden.....	70 00	....	70 00
		$6,588 70	$1,542 58	$8,131 28

Churches not reported, 11.

—o—

PRESBYTERY OF HURON.

Ministers.	Churches.	Home Objects.	General Objects.	Total.
Wm. Maclaren, D.D.......	Fostoria..............	$200 60	....	$200 00
J. K. Kost................	Plymouth.............	1,250 00	....	1,250 00
R. B. Moore..............	Tiffin.................	7,700 00	....	7,700 00
W. M. Newton............	Bloomville............	....	$558 00	558 00
W. T. Hart...............	Lyme.................	100 00	232 00	332 00
James S. McCoy..........	Sandusky	....	850 00	850 00
T. D. Bartholomew........	Olena................	460 00	105 00	565 00
James T. Pollock.........	Monroeville..........	....	....	....
Henry H. Rice............	Norwalk.............	4,512 00	....	4,512 00
T. D. Bartholomew........	Peru.................	....	80 00	80 00
W. M. Newton............	Melmore.............	....	118 00	118 00
....	Clyde................	471 00	....	471 00
....	McCutcheonville.......	....	115 00	115 00
E. Bushnell, D.D..........	Fremont..............	8,000 00	....	8,000 00
		$22,693 00	$2,058 00	$24,751 00

Churches not reported, 9.

PRESBYTERY OF LIMA.

Ministers.	Churches.	Home Objects.	General Objects.	Total.
R. H. Hollyday	Arcadia	$225 00		$225 00
Thomas Elcock	Shanesville	650 00		650 00
	Harrison	15 00	$40 00	55 00
A. B. Fields	Findlay	220 00	170 00	390 00
D. W. Cooper	Ottawa	193 00		193 00
D. W. Cooper	Wapakoneta	225 00		225 00
Wm. M. Claybaugh	Van Wert	1,778 50		1,778 50
R. McCaslin	Sidney	1,947 00		1,947 00
Samuel Carrick Kerr	Turtle Creek	300 00		300 00
	Mount Jefferson	50 00		50 00
John Daniel	Lima Union	484 00		484 00
W. A. Ward	Pleasantville	400 00		400 00
W. A. Ward	Blanchard	373 00		373 00
		$6,860 50	$210 00	$7,070 50

Churches not reported, 17.

—o—

PRESBYTERY OF MAUMEE.

Ministers.	Churches.	Home Objects.	General Objects.	Total.
P. C. Baldwin	Haskins	$2,090 00		$2,090 00
P. C. Baldwin	Mitton Centre		$5 00	5 00
J. P. P. Stockton	West Unity	750 00		750 00
J. P. P. Stockton	Mount Salem	700 00		700 00
Bernard W. Slagle	Defiance, First	1,000 00		1,000 00
Henry M. Bacon	Toledo, Westminster	16,250 00	100 00	16,350 00
G. A. Adams	Perrysburgh	975 00		975 00
G. M. Miller	Bethesda	2,000 00	10 00	2,010 00
Robert Edgar	Toledo, Second		20 00	20 00
H. N. McCracken	Toledo, First	15,535 50	115 00	15,650 50
James E. Vance	Tontogany	84 16		84 16
G. N. Todd	Delta	1,500 00		1,500 00
S. S. Hyde	Hicksville	160 00		160 00
Wm. McElwee	Bowling Green	150 00		150 00
E. Thomson	Bryan	1,781 00	10 00	1,791 00
Robert Edgar	Toledo Third	980 00		980 00
P. C. Baldwin	Weston	200 00		200 00
P. C. Baldwin	Napoleon		11 00	11 00
		$44,155 66	$271 00	$44,426 66

Churches not reported, 12.

SYNOD OF UTICA.

PRESBYTERY OF BINGHAMTON.

Ministers.	Churches.	Home Objects.	General Objects.	Total.
S. Mandeville............	Masonville............	....	$33 00	$33 00
C. O. Thatcher...........	Union, First Ch.......	$275 00	....	275 00
S. Vorhis................	Spencer...............	300 00	....	300 00
Amos Crocker.............	Coventry, Second.....	400 00	....	400 00
George N. Boardman, D.D.	Binghamton, First.....	18,000 00	5,010 00	23,010 00
C. P. Coit................	Binghamton, North....	265 00	60 00	325 00
A McMaster...............	Nichols...............	3,000 00	....	3,000 00
S. H. Howe...............	Cortland..............	1,900 00	180 00	2,080 00
W. H. Sawtell,...........	Nineveh...............	4,000 00	....	4,000 00
R. A. Clark..............	Preble................	1,000 00	....	1,000 00
....	Virgil................	500 00	....	500 00
W. R. Halbert............	Apalachin, First Ch....	425 00	....	425 00
D. D. Gregory............	Conklin...............	1,000 00	....	1,000 00
		$31,065 00	$5,283 00	$36,348 00

Churches not reported, 15.

PRESBYTERY OF OTSEGO.

Ministers.	Churches.	Home Objects.	General Objects.	Total.
Chas. Gillette............	Westford..............	$100 00	....	$100 00
J. L. Jones..............	Guilford Centre.......	....	$100 00	100 00
H. H. Allen..............	Oneonta...............	1,805 39	....	1,805 39
F. A. M. Brown...........	Delhi, Second.........	....	200 00	200 00
....	Butternutts...........	....	38 00	38 00
L. E. Richards...........	Head of Delaware......	339 00	....	339 00
P. F. Sanborn............	Springfield...........	711 00	300 00	1,011 00
Gustavus R. Alden........	Cooperstown...........	185 00	2,516 00	2,701 00
Frank H. Seely...........	Richfield Springs......	....	50 00	50 00
H. U. Swinnerton.........	Cherry Valley.........	2,000 00	33 42	2,033 42
....	Cannonsville..........	165 00	10 00	175 00
		$5,305 39	$3,247 42	$8,552 81

Churches not reported, 20.

PRESBYTERY OF ST. LAWRENCE.

Ministers.	Churches.	Home Objects.	General Objects.	Total.
....	Brasher Falls..........	$2,500 00	....	$2,500 00
E. Wood..................	Brownville............	489 08	....	489 08
James Gardner............	Canton..............	3,176 00	....	3,176 00
E. G. Bickford............	Chaumont............	1,000 00	....	1,000 00
E. Wood..................	Dexter...............	276 00	....	276 00
....	East De Kalb..........	1,280 00	....	1,280 00
....	Ellsworth............	30 00	....	30 00
N. J. Conklin............	Gouverneur..........	3,279 28	$142 25	3,421 53
R. L. McCune............	Henvelton............	600 00	....	600 00
....	Le Ray..............	2,000 00	2,716 00	4,716 00
L. M. Miller, D.D.	Oswegatchie, First.....	10,000 00	1,070 00	11,070 00
James Cleland............	Oswegatchie, Second...	....	218 00	218 00
A. Adair.................	Oxbow..............	....	44 00	44 00
Henry Hickock..	Sackett's Harbor......	270 00	....	270 00
Alex. Smith..............	Theresa	963 00	....	963 00
J. J. Porter, D.D	Watertown, First......	5,100 00	....	5,100 00
C. M. Livingston..........	Watertown, Stone St...	800 00	....	800 00
Robert W. McCormick.....	Waddington..........	114 00	....	114 00
		$31,877 36	$4,190 25	$36,067 61

Churches not reported, 14.

——o——

PRESBYTERY OF SYRACUSE.

Ministers.	Churches.	Home Objects.	General Objects.	Total.
D. Torrey, D.D	Cazenovia............	$5,314 50	....	$5,314 50
David James..............	Constantia, First Ch...	1,400 00	$526 00	1,926 00
D. W. Bigelow............	Fayetteville	3,375 00	140 00	3,515 00
....	Hannibal............	1,000 00	....	1,000 00
H. C. Hazen..............	Liverpool............	2,642 00	42 52	2,684 52
Samuel L. Merrell.........	Lysander............	250 00	....	250 00
J. A. Worden	Oswego, First.........	4,247 00	253 00	4,500 00
J. H. Frazee..............	Syracuse, First Ward..	5,738 40	200 00	5,938 40
E. G. Thurber............	Syracuse Park, Central	30,000 00	150 00	30,150 00
J. S. Bacon..............	Syracuse, Fourth......	35,000 00	....	35,000 00
E. B. Parsons.............	Baldwinsville..........	5,000 00	155 00	5,155 00
Alvin Cooper.............	Pompey..............	....	41 25	41 25
A. Robinson..............	Colamer.............	103 00	....	103 00
F. Hebard................	Amboy..............	400 00	....	400 00
H. M. Dodd..............	Manlius..............	500 00	300 00	800 00
L. R. Janes...............	Onondaga Valley......	250 00	....	250 00
A. J. Quick...............	Lenox...............	300 00	....	300 00
A. C. Shaw...............	Fulton and Granby....	3,700 00	1,600 00	5,300 00
James Marshall...........	Redfield..............	114 00	....	114 00
J. Petrie.................	Volney..............	....	20 00	20 00
		$99,333 90	3,427 77	102,761 67

Churches not reported, 15.

SYNOD OF UTICA.

PRESBYTERY OF UTICA.

Ministers.	Churches.	Home Objects.	General Objects.	Total.
P. H. Fowler, D.D........	Utica, First...........	$10,352 35	$1,473 40	$11,825 75
Thomas J. Brown.........	Utica, Westminster....	....	10,115 00	10,115 00
N. W. Goertner, D.D......	Hamilton College......	....	600 00	600 00
E. C. Pritchett............	Oriskany..............	....	100 00	100 00
George D. Baker..........	Oneida	....	1,012 12	1,012 12
A. Cochran................	Oneida Castle.........	207 00	....	207 00
V. Le Roy Lockwood......	New York Mills........	11,000 00	10,065 00	21,065 00
B. F. Willoughby...	Sauqoit...............	115 00	....	115 00
Thos. B. Hudson..........	Clinton...............	100 00	880 00	980 00
J. W. Whitfield...........	West Utica............	150 00	....	150 00
E. B. Furbish.............	New Hartford..........	6,825 14	....	6,825 14
W. M. Robinson...........	Westernville	1,969 00	....	1,969 00
E. N. Manley..............	Camden, First Church.	1,970 00	....	1,970 00
C. H. Beebe...............	Clayville..............	215 00	....	215 00
L. Williams................	Lyons Falls (Forest Ch.)	4,000 00	....	4,000 00
N. Bosworth..............	Williamstown..........	650 00	....	650 00
Peter Stryker, D.D........	Rome..................	6,800 00	300 00	7,100 00
....	Vernon................	1,000 00	....	1,000 00
W. B. Parmelee...........	Little Falls............	75 00	462 00	537 00
G. L. Roof................	Lowville..............	2,776 50	....	2,776 50
L. Williams...............	Turin..................	300 00	....	300 00
		$48,504 99	$25,007 52	$73,512 51

Churches not reported, 20.

SYNOD OF WESTERN NEW YORK.

PRESBYTERY OF GENESEE.

Ministers.	Churches.	Home Objects.	General Objects.	Total.
C. W. Hawley.............	Batavia...............	$1,264 00	$1,901 00	$3,165 00
G. S. Corwin..............	Pembroke and Batavia.	1,205 00	540 00	1,745 00
T. M. Hodgman...........	Byron.................	150 00	281 00	431 00
C. H. Taylor, D.D.........	Le Roy................	2,000 00	52,719 00	54,719 00
A. B. Morse...............	Wyoming..............	....	61 30	61 30
J. E. Nassau..............	Warsaw...............	2,480 00	212 00	2,692 00
C. W. MacCarthy...	Portageville...........	....	113 35	113 35
C. W. Remington..........	Corfu.................	387 00	....	387 00
John C. Long.............	Elba..................	1,390 00	20 00	1,410 00
....	North Bergen.........	2,238 12	50 00	2,288 12
		$11,114 12	$55,897 65	$67,011 77

PRESBYTERY OF BUFFALO.

Ministers.	Churches.	Home Objects.	General Objects.	Total.
*Walter Clark, D.D.	Buffalo, First	$13,160 00	$3,067 00	$16,227 00
John C. Lord, D.D. A. L. Benton	Buffalo, Central	....	32,775 00	32,775 00
Wolcott Calkins	Buffalo, North	10,222 97	1,069 00	11,291 97
Erskine N. White	Buffalo, Westminster	10,200 00	100 00	10,300 00
Henry Ward	Buffalo, East	2,000 00	....	2,000 00
A. D. White	Buff'o, Breckenridge St.	454 00	....	454 00
Alex. McLean	Buffalo, Calvary	4,461 97	210 00	4,671 97
S. Cowles	Gowanda	....	2,025 00	2,025 00
Ephraim Taylor	East Hamburg	375 00	....	375 00
J. M. Ballou	Clarence	100 00	....	100 00
....	Fredonia	....	20 00	20 00
Edwin S. Wright, D.D.	Ripley, First	1,100 00	....	1,100 00
....	Ripley, Second	2,400 00	....	2,400 00
Chalon Burgess	Panama	582 25	230 00	812 25
R. M. Sandford	West Aurora	500 00	....	500 00
William Waith	Lancaster	1,200 00	....	1,200 00
R. Norton	St. Catherine's, C. W.	1,500 00	2 00	1,502 00
Wm. A. Fox	Westfield	....	52 00	52 00
R. M. Sandford	East Aurora	211 00	....	211 00
W. J. Hunt	South Wales	138 00	....	138 00
		$48,605 19	$39,550 00	$88,155 19

Churches not reported, 13.

—o—

PRESBYTERY OF GENESEE VALLEY.

Ministers.	Churches.	Home Objects.	General Objects.	Total.
J. G. Ogden	Almond	$2,000 00	....	$2,000 00
John Reid	Angelica	....	$164 00	164 00
W. C. Gaylord	Burns	75 00	....	75 00
C. B. Gardner	Cuba	10,652 00	....	10,652 00
....	Franklinville	180 00	....	180 00
N. M. Clute	Olean	2,465 00	....	2,465 00
J. E. Tinker	Portville	....	160 00	160 00
John W. Lane	Rushford	500 00	53 00	553 00
		$15,872 00	$377 00	$16,249 00

*Deceased.

Churches not reported, 21.

PRESBYTERY OF NIAGARA.

Ministers.	Churches.	Home Objects.	General Objects.	Total.
W. C. Wisner, D.D........	Lockport, First........	$5,000 00	$1,000 00	$6,000 00
E. P. Marvin.............	Lockport, Second Ward	550 00	....	550 00
J. Odell..................	Lewiston........... ...	7,295 00	....	7,295 00
Thos. Doggett............	Niagara Falls.........	2,000 00	355 00	2,355 00
Wm. G. Hubbard..........	Millville..............	6,500 00	....	6,500 00
Anson G. Chester..........	Albion................	....	114 50	114 50
Edwin Hall, Jr...........	Porter or Youngstown.	700 00	....	700 00
Frederick H. Adams.......	Wilson.....	1,500 00	....	1,500 00
L. B. Rogers..............	Somerset.............	1,680 00	....	1,680 00
Samuel F. Bacon....	Carlton...	3,180 00	....	3,180 00
....	Pendleton & Wheatfield	....	....	....
C. C. Johnson.............	Holly..................	400 00	....	400 00
H. P. Bogue..............	La Salle..............	560 00	....	560 00
		$29,365 00	$1,469 50	$30,834 50

——o——

PRESBYTERY OF ROCHESTER.

Ministers.	Churches.	Home Objects.	General Objects.	Total.
J. L. Robertson...........	Rochester, First.......	$42,000 00	....	$42,000 00
James B. Shaw, D.D......	Rochester, Brick......	9,269 79	50 00	9,319 79
S. M. Campbell, D.D.......	Rochester, Central	7,159 00	7,104 72	14,263 72
....	Rochester, St. Peter's..	2,600 00		2,600 00
Henry M. Morey..........	Rochester, Westminster	3,865 76	....	3,865 76
H. W. Morris.............	Rochester, Calvary....	4,000 00	....	4,000 00
Thomas Aitken............	Sparta, First..........	121 00	136 00	257 00
Thomas Aitken............	Sparta, Second........	475 00	329 00	804 00
A. H. Corliss.............	Lima.................	1,340 00	....	1,340 00
A. Baker.................	Geneseo, First........	200 00	20 00	220 00
I. N. Sprague, D.D.......	Geneseo Village, First.	2,135 00	53 50	2,188 50
F. DeW. Ward, D.D......	Geneseo, Central......	2,459 00	150 00	2,609 00
Geo. A. Brown............	Brockport............	3,100 00	....	3,100 00
O. P. Conklin.............	Charlotte	576 00	15 00	591 00
Thomas Dobbins..........	Groveland	3,300 00	....	3,300 00
Willis C. Gaylord..........	Ossian................	42 40	....	42 40
Samuel Jessup............	Dansville	1,432 00	....	1,432 00
W. E. Jones	Tuscarora and Union Corners............	1,192 00	5 00	1,197 00
L. S. Marsh..............	Nunda...............	630 00	20 00	650 00
Geo. McCartney...........	Webster	1,100 00	....	1,100 00
J. R. Page................	E. Avon......... ...	900 00	500 00	1,400 00
Levi Parsons..............	Mt. Morris...........	700 00	122 50	822 50
Dwight Scovil.	Mendon	1,204 00	300 00	1,504 00
Alex. McA. Thorburn......	Ogden...............	....	500 00	500 00
Wm. Hunter..............	Springwater	600 00	....	600 00
S. A. Freeman............	West Mendon.........	500 00	....	500 00
....	Oakland	300 00	....	300 00
		$91,200 95	$9,305 72	$100,506 67

SYNOD OF WISCONSIN.

PRESBYTERY OF CHIPPEWA.

Ministers.	Churches.	Home Objects.	General Objects.	Total.
J. I. Smith	La Crosse, First	$425 00	....	$425 00
J. I. Smith	La Crosse, North	230 00	....	230 00
H. R. Wilson	Galesville	385 00	....	385 00
James Agnew	Hudson	300 00	....	300 00
J. M. Pryse	Big River	150 00	....	150 00
J. M. Pryse	Prescott	500 00	....	500 00
J. C. Caldwell	Neshonoc	440 00	$10 00	450 00
....	New Amsterdam	645 00	....	645 00
		$3,075 00	$10 00	$3,085 00

Churches not reported, 12.

——o——

PRESBYTERY OF WISCONSIN RIVER.

Ministers.	Churches.	Home Objects.	General Objects.	Total.
R. V. Dodge	Madison	$78 00	$226 90	$304 90
M. A. Fox	Oregon	140 00	....	140 00
E. Kudobe	Highland	....	7 30	7 30
E. Kudobe	Pulaski	....	7 50	7 50
James M. Reid	Richland City	....	18 00	18 00
W. A. Hendrickson	Columbus	850 00	....	850 00
Warren Mayo	Lodi	240 00	60 00	300 00
Wm. Lusk	Reedsburg	2,700 00	18 00	2,718 00
L. Lennard	Sun Prairie	....	30 00	30 00
W. M. Hoyt	Middleton	50 00	8 00	58 00
J. H. Ritchey	Portage City	357 25	....	357 25
A. S. Yale	Mineral Point	600 00	....	600 00
H. W. Woods	Prairie du Lac	280 05	....	280 05
C. Richards	Pardeeville	....	10 31	10 31
F. Z. Rossiter	Baraboo	530 00	10 00	540 00
G. F. Hunting	Kilbourne City	117 00	....	117 00
David S. Morgan	Montello	1,210 00	21 00	1,231 00
John U. Tschudy	Plattsville (German)	....	82 25	82 25
		$7,152 30	$499 26	$7,651 56

Churches not reported, 20.

PRESBYTERY OF LAKE SUPERIOR.

Ministers.	Churches.	Home Objects.	General Objects.	Total.
Henry S. Little............	Marquette............	....	$750 00	$750 00
A. McLachlan............	Ontonagon............	$25 00	....	25 00
N. E. Pierson...	Escanaba	77 00	25 00	102 00
W. R. Higgins............	Superior............	250 00	32 00	282 00
G. A. Little............	Oconto	130 00	....	130 00
John Fairchild............	Marinette............	4,572 23		4,572 23
		$5,054 23	$807 00	$5,861 23

——o——

PRESBYTERY OF MILWAUKEE.

Ministers.	Churches.	Home Objects.	General Objects.	Total.
A. G. Wilson.............	Beloit	$520 00	....	$520 00
T. C. Kirkwood...........	Janesville.............	1,600 00	....	1,600 00
John Martin..............	Ottawa	40 00	$3 60	43 60
E. Graham...............	Milwaukee, Calvary ...	20,405 00	....	20,405 00
J. Post, D.D.............	Milwaukee, Holland,1st	1,046 25	....	1,046 25
John Martin..............	Delafield.............	....	75 00	75 00
W. Drummond............	Stone Bank....... ...	75 00	....	75 00
J. M. Boyd..............	Barton...............	790 00	....	790 00
R. G. Thompson..........	Brodhead..............	986 00	....	986 00
C. B. Stevens.............	Manitowoc............	10,485 00	....	10,485 00
J. Gridley	Kenosha..............	126 00	....	126 00
J. Paterson..............	Cato..................	12 89	3 25	16 14
J. Kolb..................	Beloit, German........	1,269 00	10 00	1,279 00
		$37,355 14	$91 85	$37,446 99

Churches not reported, 18.

——o——

PRESBYTERY OF WINNEBAGO.

Ministers.	Churches.	Home Objects.	General Objects.	Total.
T. G. Smith	Fond du Lac..........	$1,400 00	....	$1,400 00
E. W. Garner.............	Waupaca.	150 00	....	150 00
Andrew Parsons..........	Weyauwego...........	200 00	$10 00	210 00
J. Patch..................	Amherst...	....	4 00	4 00
John E. Chapin...........	Neenah..............	1,592 18	190 00	1,782 18
....	Plover...............	....	6 00	6 00
E. Jamieson..............	Robinsonville.........	705 00	....	705 00
C. S. Wood........... ...	Stevens Point.........	....	300 00	300 00
H. L. Brown..............	Omro	600 00	....	600 00
A. G. Eagleson...........	Oshkosh........	....	13 00	13 00
T. S. Johnson............	Beaver Dam..........	250 00	50 00	300 00
		$4,897 18	$573 00	$5,470 18

SUMMARY OF THE PRESBYTERIES.

Synod.	Presbytery.	Home Objects.	General Objects.	Total.
Albany	Albany	$63,984 76	$27,381 07	$91,365 83
"	Champlain	6,609 39	66 98	6,676 37
"	Columbia	11,856 22	1,560 46	13,416 68
"	Troy	48,994 80	4,793 00	53,787 80
Atlantic	Atlantic	....	10 00	10 00
"	Catawba	200 00	407 25	607 25
"	East Florida	4,500 00	50 00	4,550 00
"	Knox	....	45 00	45 00
"	Yadkin	1,750 00	70 60	1,820 60
Baltimore	Baltimore	7,177 08	8,016 58	15,193 66
"	New Castle	94,994 76	13,836 89	108,831 65
"	Rio de Janeiro	60 15	....	60 15
"	Washington City	16,413 50	3,512 00	19,925 50
China	....	....	1,000 00	1,000 00
Cincinnati	Chillicothe	16,450 00	2,961 00	19,411 00
"	Cincinnati	43,929 91	32,553 52	76,483 43
"	Portsmouth	29,381 25	2,259 95	31,641 20
"	Dayton	40,897 07	25,948 01	66,845 08
Cleveland	Cleveland	59,922 00	85,862 15	145,784 15
"	Mahoning	67,807 85	2,100 12	69,907 97
"	St. Clairsville	17,835 00	2,547 13	20,382 13
"	Steubenville	141,910 50	64,932 10	206,842 60
Colorado	Colorado	5,334 00	63 00	5,397 00
"	Santa Fé	....	55 00	55 00
"	Wyoming	4,776 67	....	4,776 67
Columbus	Athens	5,234 75	1,632 63	6,867 38
"	Columbus	16,452 00	2,439 04	18,891 04
"	Marion	11,196 36	2,313 50	13,509 86
"	Wooster	17,600 00	13,330 21	30,930 21
"	Zanesville	11,403 00	25,063 96	36,466 96
Erie	Alleghany	24,636 18	2,880 45	27,516 63
"	Alleghany	15,171 00	340 00	15,511 00
"	Butler	9,118 08	1,208 17	10,326 25
"	Clarion	33,114 95	5,435 75	38,550 70
"	Erie	85,999 98	5,017 77	91,017 75
"	Kittanning	31,984 95	8,281 45	40,266 40
"	Shenango	7,117 25	2,883 19	10,000 44
Geneva	Cayuga	70,020 60	24,555 30	94,575 90
"	Chemung	13,900 00	7,674 00	21,574 00
"	Geneva	55,638 50	4,566 00	60,204 50
"	Steuben	44,481 56	476 00	44,957 56
"	Lyons	31,263 00	1,466 50	32,729 50
Harrisburgh	Carlisle	68,470 33	17,680 00	86,150 33
"	Huntingdon	82,890 82	7,919 65	90,810 47
"	Northumberland	89,569 84	4,888 71	94,458 55
"	Wellsboro	11,467 00	50 00	11,517 00
Illinois Central	Bloomington	33,676 75	1,751 96	35,428 71
"	Peoria	26,976 29	2,872 65	29,848 94
"	Schuyler	20,801 02	2,388 00	23,189 02
"	Springfield	63,982 00	11,430 00	75,412 00
Illinois North	Chicago	101,378 85	60,905 55	62,284 40
"	Freeport	33,735 75	2,219 14	35,954 89
"	Ottawa	23,650 68	1,034 00	24,684 68
"	Rock River	26,239 79	1,893 10	28,132 89
Illinois South	Alton	45,655 55	1,004 20	46,469 75
"	Cairo	16,844 25	2,778 00	19,622 25
"	Mattoon	34,544 75	350 00	34,894 75

Continued on next page.

SUMMARY OF THE PRESBYTERIES.—CONTINUED.

Synod.	Presbytery.	Home Objects.	General Objects.	Total.
Indiana North	Crawfordsville	$52,723 82	$12,561 68	$65,285 50
"	Fort Wayne	14,226 00	5,071 00	19,297 00
"	Logansport	30,866 00	800 00	32,666 00
"	Muncie	20,302 00	685 50	20,987 50
Indiana South	Indianapolis	71,348 53	45,422 79	116,771 32
"	New Albany	39,950 50	24,623 65	64,574 15
"	Vincennes	30,507 94	3,442 00	33,949 94
"	White Water	30,119 22	994 00	31,113 22
Iowa North	Cedar Rapids	18,383 82	2,133 52	20,517 34
"	Dubuque	10,222 57	3,087 92	13,310 49
"	Fort Dodge	1,805 00	....	1,805 00
Iowa South	Waterloo	12,208 75	340 00	12,548 75
"	Des Moines	20,044 00	28,699 50	48,743 50
"	Iowa	10,239 50	45 00	10,284 50
"	Iowa City	11,951 50	2,626 00	14,577 50
"	Missouri River	31,115 36	450 00	31,565 36
Kansas	Emporia	8,565 00	242 40	8,807 40
"	Highland	6,156 00	5,685 00	11,841 50
"	Neosho	10,297 00	90 00	10,387 00
"	Topeka	40,991 50	485 00	41,476 50
Kentucky	Ebenezer	45,923 43	9,348 50	55,271 93
"	Louisville	8,475 00	4,410 00	12,885 00
"	Transylvania	6,137 85	516 00	6,653 85
Long Island	Brooklyn	105,995 57	3,836 00	109,831 57
"	Long Island	11,415 22	303 99	11,719 21
"	Nassau	22,150 72	1,608 00	23,758 72
Michigan	Detroit	60,199 13	12,326 75	72,525 88
"	Grand Rapids	13,369 75	265 84	13,635 59
"	Kalamazoo	6,411 53	4,342 50	10,754 03
"	Lansing	3,194 00	1,813 50	5,007 50
"	Monroe	29,385 47	111 00	29,496 47
"	Saginaw	8,398 16	371 00	8,769 16
Minnesota	Mankato	23,761 00	242 50	24,003 50
"	St. Paul	58,870 01	3,618 00	62,188 61
"	Winona	8,371 70	50 00	8,421 70
Missouri	Osage	12,466 60	235 00	12,701 60
"	Ozark	13,909 55	....	13,909 55
"	Palmyra	12,289 00	20,026 00	32,315 00
"	Platte	16,654 00	15 00	16,669 00
"	Potosi	3,029 50	11 00	3,040 50
"	St. Louis	70,564 05	32,831 00	103,395 05
New Jersey	Elizabeth	99,067 30	13,227 90	112,295 20
"	Jersey City	20,131 81	13,588 00	33,719 81
"	Monmouth	42,734 33	2,606 15	45,340 48
"	Morris and Orange	127,953 30	24,972 03	152,925 33
"	Newark	73,211 88	31,708 66	104,920 54
"	New Brunswick	30,413 75	16,445 76	46,859 51
"	Newton	63,108 77	16,464 43	79,573 20
"	West Jersey	50,458 50	4,620 00	55,078 50
New York	Boston	12,377 98	1,736 50	14,114 48
"	Hudson	26,583 00	2,280 80	28,863 80
"	New York	285,718 58	498,618 45	784,337 03
"	North River	48,462 87	2,085 30	50,548 17
"	Westchester	111,870 75	11,082 05	122,952 80
Pacific	Benicia	14,469 50	400 00	14,869 50
"	Oregon	2,855 50	308 75	3,164 25
"	Sacramento	22,527 00	735 00	23,262 00
"	San Francisco	81,537 50	5,337 90	86,875 40
"	San José	19,610 00	172 00	19,782 00
Philadelphia	Chester	60,530 26	4,631 10	65,161 36
"	Lackawanna	67,015 30	32,290 75	100,306 05
"	Lehigh	58,944 05	7,135 19	66,079 24
"	Philadelphia	116,789 95	32,111 40	148,901 35
"	Philadelphia Central	251,450 58	9,151 70	260,602 28
"	Philadelphia North	76,941 01	9,820 22	86,761 23
"	Westminster	63,876 29	1,404 00	65,280 29

Continued on next page.

SUMMARY OF THE PRESBYTERIES.—CONTINUED.

Synod.	Presbytery.	Home Objects.	General Objects.	Total.
Pittsburgh	Blairsville	$16,327 00	$4,182 95	$20,509 95
"	Pittsburgh	83.304 99	87,474 08	170,779 07
"	Redstone	55,775 00	3,183 00	58,958 00
"	Washington	42,136 16	10,254 44	52,390 60
"	West Virginia	3,058 00	1,856 96	4,914 96
Tennessee	Austin	4,000 00	40 00	4,040 00
"	Holston	1,988 00	79 41	2,067 41
"	Kingston	2,073 00	1,715 00	3,788 00
"	New Orleans	....	123 75	123 75
"	Union	7,358 70	572 49	7,931 19
Toledo	Belfontaine	6,988 70	1,542 58	8,531 28
"	Huron	22,693 00	2,058 00	24,751 00
"	Lima	6,860 50	210 00	7,070 50
"	Maumee	44,155 66	271 00	44,426 66
Utica	Binghamton	31,065 00	5,283 00	36,348 00
"	Otsego	5,305 39	3,247 42	8,552 81
"	St. Lawrence	31,877 36	4,190 25	36,067 61
"	Syracuse	99,333 90	3,427 77	102,761 67
"	Utica	48,504 99	25,007 52	73,512 51
Western New York	Buffalo	48,605 19	39,550 00	88,155 19
" "	Genesee	11,114 12	55,897 65	67,011 77
" "	Genesee Valley	15,872 00	377 00	16,249 00
" "	Niagara	29,365 00	1,469 50	30,834 50
" "	Rochester	91,200 95	9,305 72	100,506 67
Wisconsin	Chippewa	3,075 00	10 00	3,085 00
"	Lake Superior	5,054 23	807 00	5,861 23
"	Winnebago	4,897 18	573 00	5,470 18
"	Wisconsin River	7,152 30	499 26	7,651 56
"	Milwaukee	37,355 14	91 85	37,446 99
Total of all the Presbyteries		$5,734,325 21	$1,828,197 77	$7,202,523 00

RECAPITULATION.

FROM CHURCHES, ... { HOME OBJECTS.....$5,374,225 21 / GENERAL OBJECTS...1,823,197 79 } $7,202,523 00

INDIVIDUAL AND MISCELLANEOUS GIFTS, MOSTLY FOR GENERAL OBJECTS.......... 631,460 85

TOTAL.............................. $7,833,983 85

ABSTRACT OF REPORT OF HON. WM. E. DODGE, TREASURER PRESBYTERIAN MEMORIAL FUND, AUGUST 1st, 1871.

1871.			1871.		
August 1.	Amount of Receipts to date	$114,574 11	August 1.	Appropriations paid by order of Committee, viz. :—	
				For New Churches	$30,876 44
				" Colleges and Theological Seminaries	12,223 47
				" Institutions in Foreign Lands	26,517 60
				" " among Freedmen	4,982 00
				" Special Gifts to the Boards	10,943 66
				" Church among Seminoles	1,000 00
				" Chinese in California	619 50
				" Presbyterian House in New York	260 00
				" Churches among the Indians	1,000 00
				" Presbyterian Hospital	175 28
					$88,597 95
				" Expenses incurred by the Committee	12,675 63
				Balance on hand, mostly appropriated but not distributed	13,300 53
		$114,574 11			$114,574 11

The Treasurer's Acc'ts were audited up to the meeting of the last Assembly. They will again be audited in the final Report presented to the Assembly of 1872.

LIST OF WOOD ENGRAVINGS.

1. TITLE PAGE.
2. FAC-SIMILE CERTIFICATE OF REUNION. Signed by the two Moderators and seven Clerks of 1869.
3. THE FIRST CHURCH, PHILADELPHIA. Where the Assembly of 1870 convened.
4. CHURCH OF THE COVENANT, NEW YORK. Where the Assembly (N. S.) of 1869 convened.
5. BRICK CHURCH, NEW YORK. Where the Assembly (O. S.) of 1869 convened.
6. PORTRAITS OF THE COMMITTEE OF CONFERENCE—MINISTERS, (O.S.), VIZ.:
   Rev. G. W. MUSGRAVE, D.D., LL.D. Rev. L. H. ATWATER, D.D.
   Rev. A. G. HALL, D.D. Rev. WILLIS LORD, D.D.
   Rev. H. R. WILSON, D.D.
7. PORTRAITS OF THE COMMITTEE OF CONFERENCE—LAYMEN, (O. S.), VIZ.:
   ROBERT CARTER, Esq. Hon. W. M. FRANCIS.
   J. C. GRIER, Esq. Hon. C. D. DRAKE.
   HENRY DAY, Esq.
8. PORTRAITS OF THE COMMITTEE OF CONFERENCE—MINISTERS, (N. S.), VIZ.:
   Rev. WILLIAM ADAMS, D.D., LL.D. Rev. R. W. PATTERSON, D.D.
   Rev. J. F. STEARNS, D.D. Rev. S. W. FISHER, D.D., LL.D.
   Rev. J. B. SHAW, D.D.
9. PORTRAITS OF THE COMMITTEE OF CONFERENCE—LAYMEN, (N. S.), VIZ.:
   Hon. WILLIAM STRONG. Hon. DANIEL HAINES.
   Hon. WILLIAM E. DODGE. J. S. FARRAND, Esq.
   JOHN L. KNIGHT, Esq.
10. A COMMUNION GATHERING IN THE OLDEN TIME.
11. AUBURN SEMINARY.
12. PORTRAIT OF REV. ASHBEL GREEN, D.D., LL.D.
13. PORTRAIT OF REV. JAMES RICHARDS, D.D.
14. THIRD CHURCH, PITTSBURGH, PA.
15. FIRST CHURCH, PITTSBURGH, PA.
16. OLD PRINCETON COLLEGE.

SOLD EXCLUSIVELY BY SUBSCRIPTION.

The permanent value of the volume is enhanced by statistical and biographical matter that will have lasting interest, from the pens of the Rev. E. F. HATFIELD, D.D., *Stated Clerk of the General Assembly*, and Rev. DAVID IRVING, D.D., *Secretary of the Board of Foreign Missions*, and Rev. J. H. M. KNOX, D.D.

STYLES AND PRICES.

English Cloth	*$3 50*	*Half Calf and Half Mor.*	*$6 00*
English Cloth, gilt edges	*4 50*	*Full Turkey Morocco, Antique*	*8 00*
Sheep	*4 50*		

SENT FREE OF EXPENSE ON RECEIPT OF THE PRICE.

DE WITT C. LENT & CO., Publishers,

451 BROOME STREET, N. Y.

A Pamphlet containing Testimonials descriptive of the work can be had, gratis, on application.

www.ingramcontent.com/pod-product-compliance
Lightning Source LLC
LaVergne TN
LVHW021426110826
845150LV00007B/2101

9781425508203